my revision notes

OCR GCSE
DESIGN and TECHNOLOGY:
Food Technology

**Val Fehners, Barbara DiNicoli
and Meryl Simpson**

HODDER
EDUCATION
AN HACHETTE UK COMPANY

Photo credits: Figure 1.1 Elena Schweitzer – Fotolia; Figure 1.3 © Crown Copyright, reproduced under the Open Government Licence, source: Department of Health in association with the Welsh Assembly Government, the Scottish Government and the Food Standards Agency in Northern Ireland; Figure 2.1 © Photolibrary Group; Figure 2.2 Comugnero Silvana – Fotolia; Figure 2.5 Igor Dutina – Fotolia; Figure 3.1 Photolibrary Group; Figure 3.2 © Stockbyte/Getty Images Ltd; Figure 4.1 Shariff Che'Lah – Fotolia; Figure 4.2 Karen Struthers – Fotolia; Figure 6.2 Coeliac UK; Figure 6.4 www.oatly.co.uk, reproduced with permission; Figure 10.1 Tesco Value Unsalted Butter and Tesco Value Lard © Tesco Stores Limited; Figure 10.3 © Unilever; Figure 10.5 Tesco Vegetable Oil and Tesco Olive Oil © Tesco Stores Limited; Figure 11.1 © Igor Dutina – Fotolia.com; Figure 12.1© Imagestate Media (John Foxx); Figure 12.2 © Imagestate Media (John Foxx); Figure 12.3 © Purestock; Figure 12.4 ©Klaus Tiedge/iStockphoto.com; Figure 12.6 Yuri Arcurs – Fotolia; Figure 13.4 Coeliac UK; Figure 15.1 © Andrew Callaghan; Figure 15.2 Photolibrary Group; Figure 17.1a © Kelpfish - Fotolia.com; Figure 17.1b Ingram; Figure 17.1c © Steve Lovegrove - Fotolia.com; Figure 17.2c © sylvie peruzzi – Fotolia.com; Figure 18.2 © Andrew Callaghan; Figure 18.3 Lana Smith – Fotolia; Figure 20.1 photocrew – Fotolia; Figure 20.2 © Chris Dascher/iStockphoto.com; Figure 21.1 © Ingram Publishing Company/Ultimate Food Photography; Figure 21.3 © Ernesto Solla Domínguez/iStockphoto.com; Figure 22.2 Rafa Irusta – Fotolia; Figure 23.1 © 2008 kamel ADJENEF/iStockphoto.com; Figure 23.2 © Crown copyright. Contains public sector information licensed under the Open Government Licence v1.0; Figure 26.1 © Bananastock/Photolibrary Group Ltd/Getty Images; Figure 26.2 Eric Gevaert – Fotolia; Figure 27.2 © Dr. Heinz Linke/iStockphoto.com; Figure 28.1 © Stockbyte/Getty Images Ltd; Figure 28.2 Martin Nemec – Fotolia; Figure 28.3 © Ingram Publishing Limited; Figure 28.4 SemA – Fotolia; Figure 31.1 © Bon Appetit/ Alamy; Figure 32.3 Martin Turzak – Fotolia; Figure 32.4 .shock – Fotolia; Figure 33.1 Fairtrade Foundation; Figure 33.2 Traidcraft; Figure 33.3 Assured Food Standards; Figure 33.5 Soil Association; Figure 34.1 Digital Vision/Photodisc/Getty Images; Figure 35.2 LobsteR – Fotolia; Figure 35.3 © Dena Steiner/iStockphoto.com; Figure 36.1 © Imagestate Media (John Foxx).

All other photos taken by the authors.

Every effort has been made to trace and acknowledge the ownership of copyright material. If any sources remain inadvertently unacknowledged the publishers will be glad to make suitable arrangements at the earliest opportunity.

Orders: please contact Bookpoint Ltd, 130 Milton Park, Abingdon, Oxon OX14 4SB. Telephone: +44 (0)1235 827720. Fax: +44 (0)1235 400454. Lines are open from 9.00a.m. to 5.00p.m., Monday–Saturday, with a 24-hour message-answering service. You can also order through our website: www.hoddereducation.co.uk

If you have any comments to make about this, or any of our other titles, please send them to educationenquiries@hodder.co.uk

British Library Cataloguing in Publication Data
A catalogue record for this title is available from the British Library

ISBN: 978 1 4441 67 22 1
This Edition Published 2012
Impression number 10 9 8 7 6 5 4 3 2 1
Year 2017, 2016, 2015, 2014, 2013, 2012

Hachette UK's policy is to use papers that are natural, renewable and recyclable products and made from wood grown in sustainable forests. The logging and manufacturing processes are expected to conform to the environmental regulations of the country of origin.

Cover photo xiangdong Li – Fotolia
Typeset by Datapage, India
Printed in Spain for Hodder Education, an Hachette UK Company, 338 Euston Road, London NW1 3BH

Contents

	☑	☑	
	Revised	Tested	

Get the most from this book

Planning your revision

Everyone has to decide their own revision strategy, but it is essential to review your work, learn key facts and test your understanding. This book will help you to do that in a planned way, topic by topic. You can check your progress by ticking off each section as you revise.

Tick to track your progress

Use the Revision planner on pages iii and iv to plan your revision, topic by topic. Tick each box when you have:

1 revised and understood a topic

2 tested yourself

3 practised the exam questions.

You can also keep track of your revision by ticking off each topic heading in the book. You may find it helpful to add your own notes as you work through each topic.

Features to help you succeed

Each topic is divided into sections that provide the information that you need to know.

Contents

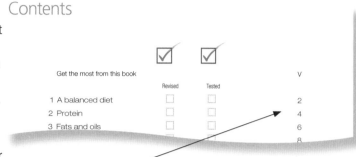

Examiner tip

Throughout the book there are tips from examiners to help you boost your grade. These identify the typical mistakes candidates make and explain how you can avoid them.

Glossary

Key words are shown in bold on the pages where they appear. You will find clear, concise definitions of these key words in the Glossary at the end of the book.

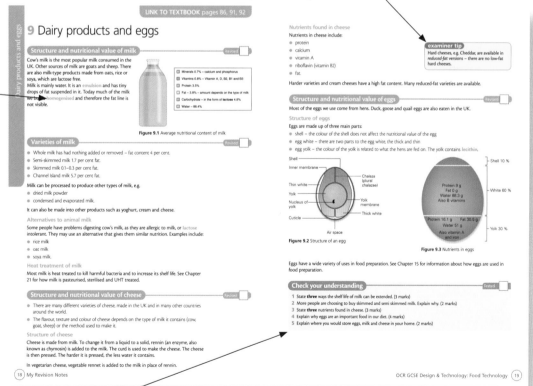

Check your understanding

These are short, knowledge-based, exam-style questions to provide the first step in testing your learning. They appear at the end of each chapter. Use them to make sure that you have understood every topic. You will find the answers to these questions in a separate section at the end of the book.

Your teacher will be able to provide you with more exam questions from previous examinations.

> Remember: the more practice questions you do, the better you will do in your examination!

The examinations up to June 2013

There are two examination papers:

- A522 Sustainable Design (one hour)
- A524 Technical Aspects of Designing and Making (one hour and 15 minutes)

For your A522 examination you will only need to revise the chapters in this book related to sustainable design (Chapters 32–36).

For your A524 examination you will need to revise *all* the chapters, as the examination could include questions on any of the topics covered in this book.

The examinations in 2014 and onwards

If you are sitting your GCSE examinations in Summer 2014, you will have just one examination. The examination could include any of the information from this book.

It will be one hour and 30 minutes long and consist of two sections:

- Section A: 15 short-word questions and one 20-mark question based on sustainable design
- Section B: three 15-mark questions, which will include design.

Banded marked questions

Look out for questions marked with (*). The way you write your answers to these questions is important – you will be marked on the quality of your written communication. This means that you must structure your answer carefully and use the correct technical terms, as well as applying your knowledge.

Design

Every year there are design questions. You may be asked to adapt a recipe, or design a completely new one.

It is important to show clearly how your design meets the specification that you have been given in the question. For example, just stating that the product contains vegetables will not gain a mark. You need to state the name of each vegetable, explain why it is used and state the specification point that it meets.

Examination reminder

Note the date, time and location of your examinations in the spaces below.

For examinations up to June 2013

Food Technology – Sustainable Design (A522) (one hour)

Date: ....

Time: ....

Location: ....

Food Technology – Technical Aspects of Designing and Making (A524) (one hour, 15 minutes)

Date: ....

Time: ....

Location: ....

For examinations in 2014 and onwards (one hour, 30 minutes)

Date: ....

Time: ....

Location: ....

1 A balanced diet

A healthy **balanced diet** is one that contains the correct combination of food and **nutrients** to grow and keep healthy.

Why do we need food? — Revised

Every living thing needs food – it is essential to keep us alive and in good health. We need food for all the following reasons:

- to provide the energy we need to survive, to keep us healthy and to help fight disease
- for growth and repair of body tissues
- for all bodily functions, which depend upon the energy that food provides
- to stop us feeling hungry
- to keep us content, as eating is a pleasurable experience.

Figure 1.1 We need a range of healthy foods as part of our balanced diet

What are nutrients? — Revised

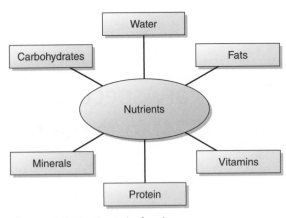

Figure 1.2 Nutrients in food

Nutrients are substances found in foods. All foods contain a mix of nutrients. Nutrients are divided into two types:

- **macronutrients** (fats, proteins and carbohydrates) – these are needed by the body in relatively large quantities and form the bulk of our diet.
- **micronutrients** (vitamins and minerals) – these are found in food and are vital to health, but are required in very small quantities.

We also need two other important substances. These are:

- water, which is found in foods and drinks
- fibre, which is found in plant foods.

Government guidelines — Revised

The UK Government has produced **dietary guidelines** and advice to encourage the UK population to improve our diet and lifestyle.

It sets targets to reduce the numbers of people with diet-related medical conditions, such as some cancers, coronary heart disease (CHD), strokes, Type 2 diabetes and **obesity**. It advises us to reduce fat, salt, sugar and alcohol and to increase fibre in our diet.

The Eatwell plate

Figure 1.3 The Eatwell plate (Source: Department of Health in association with the Welsh Assembly Government, the Scottish Government and the Food Standards Agency in Northern Ireland)

This is a food guide in the form of an image of a plate of food. It shows the proportion and types of foods that are needed to make up a healthy, balanced diet.

It encourages us to choose foods from:

- fruit and vegetables (at least five portions)
- bread, potatoes, rice and pasta (plenty)
- milk and other dairy products (some)
- meat, fish, eggs and beans (some)

It shows that we should eat only a small amount of foods that are high in fat and/or sugar.

The '5 a day' campaign

This campaign:

- encourages us to eat more fruit and vegetables – fresh, frozen, canned and dried
- ensures a variety of vitamins, minerals, trace elements and fibre in the diet
- promotes the inclusion of antioxidants and plant chemicals, which are needed for good health.

Check your understanding ────────────────────── Tested ☐

1 State **two** dangers of having a poor diet. (2 marks)
2 State how the following packed lunch could be improved to meet the Eatwell plate guidance: white bread with chocolate spread, packet of crisps, can of Coke and a chocolate bar. (4 marks)
3 Give **one** reason why we should reduce the amount of salt we eat. (1 mark)
4 State **two** alternatives to using salt to flavour foods. (2 marks)
5 List **six** ways that secondary schools could encourage teenagers to eat a healthy diet. (6 marks)

Protein

2 Protein

What are proteins? Revised

Protein is one of the macronutrients essential for growth and repair of body tissue, and is crucial to the healthy functioning of the body. Protein is made up of complex chains of molecules called amino acids. There are 20 different types of amino acid, each with a specific function in the body.

Functions and sources of protein in the diet Revised

Functions of protein in the diet

- Growth, especially in children and pregnant women.
- Repair body tissue after illness, accidents and surgery for people of all ages.
- Enzymes and hormones are composed of proteins.
- Provide a secondary source of energy. When the body has used all the amino acids it needs for construction, the remainder are 'burnt' for energy.

Sources

Animal sources include all meats, such as poultry, offal and game, as well as fish, cheese, milk, eggs and gelatine.

> **examiner tip**
> Growth and repair of cells counts as two separate answers.

Figure 2.1 Animal sources of protein

Figure 2.2 Vegetable proteins

Vegetable sources include soya beans and soya products, pulses, beans, cereal grains and cereal products, nuts and Quorn®.

Amino acids Revised

The human body needs all 20 amino acids for the maintenance of health and growth. Some of these can be made by the body itself, but the others have to be obtained through the food we eat – these are called essential amino acids. There are eight essential amino acids for adults and ten for children.

High biological value (HBV) proteins

Foods that contain all the essential amino acids are said to have a high biological value (HBV). Most of these come from animal sources.

Low biological value (LBV) proteins

These do not contain all the essential amino acids and are said to have low biological value (LBV).

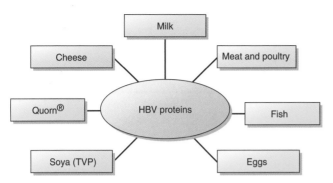

Figure 2.3 High biological value proteins

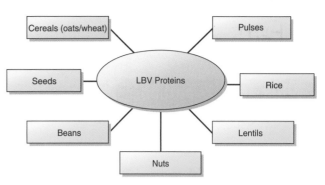

Figure 2.4 Low biological value proteins

Food combining

Revised

Vegetarian, vegan or other limited diets rely on combining LBV proteins to form proteins of higher value. This is called food combining or eating complementary proteins.

Examples are:

- beans on toast
- dhal and rice
- hummus and pitta bread.

Figure 2.5 Vegetarian sources of protein

Check your understanding

Tested

1 State **three** functions of protein in the diet. (3 marks)
2 State the meaning of the term 'essential amino acids'. (1 mark)
3 Give the name of one vegetable protein that provides all the essential amino acids. (1 mark)
4 State **two** products that would give a vegan all the essential amino acids. (2 marks)
5 State **one** source of protein for each of the following target groups:
    – toddler
    – lacto-vegetarian
    – elderly person. (3 marks)

3 Fats and oils

What are fats and oils?

- 'Lipids' is a general term for both fats and oils.
- Oils are fats that are liquid at room temperature.
- All fats and oils have similar chemical structures and functions.
- All fats are high in calories.
- Our fat intake should be no more than 35 per cent of our total energy intake.
- Fat in the diet is important for health and wellbeing.
- Excess fat in the diet is stored as body fat.

The functions and sources of fat in the diet

Functions of fat in the diet

- Fat is a source of energy.
- It forms part of the structure of cells.
- Stored under the skin, fat helps insulate the body against the cold.
- Our vital organs, such as kidneys, are protected by a layer of fat.
- It is a source of the fat-soluble vitamins A, D, E and K (see also Chapter 5, on vitamins).
- It provides essential fatty acids for the structure and function of body cells.
- We like to eat fat because it gives foods texture and flavour.
- Fat in our diet helps to promote a feeling of **satiety** (feeling full after eating).

> **examiner tip**
>
> Make sure that you know at least one other function of fat as well as providing energy.

Sources

Fats come from both plant and animal sources.

Plant	Animal
Fruits (e.g. avocado, olives)	Meat and meat products (e.g. lard, suet)
Nuts and pulses (e.g. peanuts, walnuts)	Dairy products (e.g. milk, butter, cheese)
Seeds (e.g. sesame, sunflower)	Oily fish (e.g. tuna, salmon, sardines)

Table 3.1 Plant and animal sources of fat

Visible and invisible fats

- Some fats are visible, such as the fat on meat or solid fats such as butter.
- Other fats form part of the food product and cannot be seen, such as in ready meals, chocolate, biscuits and burgers.

Figure 3.1 Visible fats and oils

Figure 3.2 Processed foods contain invisible fats

The chemistry of fats

- **Saturated fats** are solid at room temperature and are mainly found in animal foods. Too much saturated fat in the diet has been linked to high blood **cholesterol,** leading to an increased risk of coronary heart disease, diabetes and obesity.
- **Monounsaturated fats** are found in both animal and vegetable fats. Monounsaturated fatty acids in particular are considered healthier because they can help to lower blood cholesterol.
- **Polyunsaturated fats** are very soft or oily at room temperature. They will not go solid even in the refrigerator. They are preferred in the diet.
- **Essential fatty acids** (EFAs) cannot be made by the body but are important to the healthy and efficient functioning of the body. They are essential for regulating body processes, including blood clotting and control of inflammation. Two important ones are:
  - *Omega* 3, found in oily fish, seeds, walnut oil, and green leafy vegetables. It helps to protect the heart.
  - *Omega* 6, found in vegetables, fruits, grains, chicken and seeds. It helps lower cholesterol in the blood.

Check your understanding

1 Give **four** functions of fat in the diet. (4 marks)
2 Give **two** reasons why high-fat food products appeal to us. (4 marks)
3 List **four** reasons why we should cut down on the amount of saturated fats that we eat. (4 marks)
4 Give **one** reason why a high-fat diet leads to obesity. (1 mark)
5 Explain the link between fats in the diet and heart disease. (4 marks)

4 Carbohydrate

Figure 4.1 Athletes need a diet that is high in carbohydrates

Figure 4.2 Carbohydrate foods

Functions and types of carbohydrate

Revised ☐

Functions of carbohydrate in the diet

- Provides the body with energy for physical activity.
- Provides the body with energy to maintain bodily functions.
- Provides dietary fibre (non-starch polysaccharide (NSP)) to help digestion.
- Sweetens and flavours foods.

If we eat more carbohydrates than we need for energy, the excess is stored as fat.

The most common problems of excess carbohydrates in the body are related to obesity and tooth decay.

Types of carbohydrates

They are divided into sugars and starches, also known as simple and complex carbohydrates.

> **examiner tip**
>
> Remember that the only function of sugar in the diet is energy. It does not contain any other nutrients.

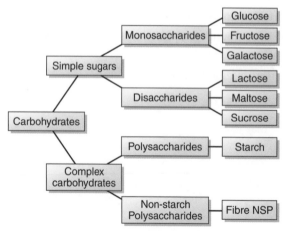

Figure 4.3 Simple and complex carbohydrates

Sugar and tooth decay

Revised

We eat sugar in different forms:

- **intrinsic sugars**, which are found naturally in the cells of fruits and vegetables
- **extrinsic sugars**, which are those you can see (such as cane sugar) and are added to cakes, biscuits, desserts and sweets.

Tooth decay is caused when the bacteria in your mouth (**plaque**) feeds on sucrose to produce an acid. The acid then causes small holes in your teeth (**dental caries**).

Plaque + sucrose = acid ➜ Acid + tooth = decay

Complex carbohydrates (starch polysaccharides)

Revised

Starch is found in grain products like bread, rice, cereals and pasta, and in some fruits and vegetables. Starches take longer than sugars for the body to digest and so provide a feeling of fullness for longer, helping to avoid over-eating and obesity. All starch comes from plant sources.

Functions of starch in the diet

- It is broken down slowly into simple sugars by the digestive system to provide a slow release of energy.
- It adds bulk to our diet.
- It gives a feeling of fullness.
- The excess is converted to fat.

Dietary fibre (non-starch polysaccharide)

Revised

Dietary fibre is the non-digestible cellulose found in plant foods.

It cannot be digested so it passes straight through the digestive system, absorbing moisture and providing bulk. We should be eating no less than 18 g of fibre a day.

Functions of dietary fibre

- It holds water and keeps the faeces soft and bulky.
- It helps to 'push' other food through the system and helps to 'clean' the walls of the intestine of bacteria.
- It helps prevent various bowel disorders, including constipation, bowel cancer, **diverticular disease**, appendicitis and haemorrhoids (piles).
- It can help people to control their body weight because high-fibre foods are filling.
- High-fibre diets are linked to lower blood cholesterol.

examiner tip

There is no fibre in sugar!

Good sources of soluble fibre are oats, peas, beans, lentils, most types of fruit and vegetables. Vegetables and fruits also provide more fibre if eaten unpeeled.

Check your understanding

Tested

1 Give **three** functions of carbohydrates in the diet. (3 marks)
2 Explain why we are encouraged to eat intrinsic sugars instead of extrinsic sugars. (4 marks)
3 State **two** reasons why it is important to include dietary fibre in the diet. (2 marks)
4 List **two** foods that are a good source of dietary fibre. (2 marks)
5 Name **two** health conditions which may be caused by a intake of low dietary fibre. (2 marks)

5 Vitamins, minerals and water

Why we need vitamins and minerals in the diet

Vitamins and minerals are micronutrients – so called because they are needed only in very small quantities. Vitamins and minerals are essential to the body to maintain health, help prevent deficiency diseases, regulate repair of body cells, bones and teeth, help process carbohydrates and release energy in the body, control body processes, especially the nervous system, contribute towards healthy body fluids, cells and blood.

examiner tip

Vitamins and minerals do not provide energy.

Vitamins

There are two main groups of vitamins, fat-soluble and water-soluble.

Fat-soluble vitamins	Function (its job) in the body)	Good sources
Vitamin A	Keeps eyes healthy and improves night vision Helps maintain skin	Liver, oily fish, eggs, milk, cheese and butter, margarine
Vitamin D	Works with calcium to build and maintain strong bones and teeth	Dairy products, oily fish, liver, cereals. Also exposure to sunlight

Table 5.1 Functions and sources of fat-soluble Vitamins A and D in the diet

Water-soluble vitamins	Function (its job) in the body)	Good sources
B group	Normal growth; healthy skin; release of energy	Fortified breakfast cereals, meat, eggs, milk, cereals, yeast and yeast extract
Vitamin C	Formation of connective tissue; helps wound healing and calcium absorption; helps absorb iron	Citrus and soft fruits, blackcurrants, green vegetables (e.g. cabbage)

Table 5.2 Functions and sources of water-soluble Vitamins B and C in the diet

Minerals

Mineral/element	Function in the body	Good sources
Iron	Found in haemoglobin in red blood cells, which carry oxygen in the blood Formation of red blood cells	Red meat, kidneys, liver Eggs, bread Green vegetables

continued on next page

Mineral/element	Function in the body	Good sources
Calcium	Hardens bones and teeth Blood clotting Heart regulation Nerve and muscle function	Dairy products, white bread Oily fish, green vegetables Nuts/seeds, Citrus fruits
Phosphorus	Works with calcium to harden bones and teeth Contributes to muscle function	Dairy products, nuts, meat Fish, foods rich in calcium
Sodium	Maintains water balance in the body Used in nerve transmission	Cheese, bacon, fish, processed foods, table salt
Fluoride	Strengthens teeth against decay	Fish, tea, drinking water

Table 5.3 The functions and sources of minerals

Functions of water in the body
Revised

- Water helps regulate body temperature. Sweat evaporates and cools us. Without this cooling system we would become ill from heat stroke.
- It helps the kidneys flush out harmful excess or foreign substances from our blood.
- It transports nutrients, oxygen and carbon dioxide round the body.
- Water is needed by nearly all body processes, e.g. digestion.
- There must be a balance between input and output of water or dehydration will occur.

Check your understanding
Tested

1 Give the name of one mineral or vitamin with the following function:
   a) helps form strong bones
   b) needed for the formation of blood cells
   c) aids night vision
   d) needed for the release of energy from our food
   e) helps wounds heal. (5 marks)
2 State **one** vitamin that aids the absorption of calcium. (1 mark)
3 Give the names of **two** fat-soluble vitamins. (2 marks)
4 State **one** mineral that is found in the following foods:
   a) cheese
   b) beef
   c) packet of crisps
   d) drinking water. (4 marks)
5 State **four** functions of water in the diet. (4 marks)

Cereals

6 Cereals

Cereals are often the staple food within a country because they are cheap to produce in comparison to protein foods. The main types of cereal foods are:

- wheat
- rice
- maize
- oats
- barley
- rye.

Wheat ————————————————————————————————— Revised ☐

Wheat is made into flour. Flours can be described by their extraction rate, i.e. how much of the whole grain is used, as shown in Table 6.1.

Flour	Extraction rate	Other important information
Wholemeal flour	100 per cent	Light brown in colour
Brown flour	85–95 per cent	Light brown in colour
White flour	70–75 per cent	The bran, germ, fat and some of the minerals have been removed. Under UK law, white flour has to be **fortified** with iron, calcium, thiamine and niacin.

Table 6.1 Extraction rates of flours

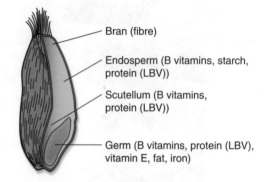

- Bran (fibre)
- Endosperm (B vitamins, starch, protein (LBV))
- Scutellum (B vitamins, protein (LBV))
- Germ (B vitamins, protein (LBV), vitamin E, fat, iron)

Figure 6.1 Structure of wheat and nutrients found in it

All flours are fortified with calcium, iron, thiamine and niacin. A large range of flours is available in supermarkets.

Flour	Important information	Uses
Strong plain flour	Higher gluten content.	Bread-making, flaky, choux and puff pastry
Soft plain flour	Has a lower gluten content	Cakes and shortcrust and suet crust pastry
Self-raising flour	Has a lower gluten content and a chemical raising agent added	Cakes, scones
Gluten-free flour	The protein removed from the flour. It is made for people who have coeliac disease.	

Table 6.2 The main types of flour

Rice ————————————————————————————————— Revised ☐

Rice is a good source of:

- carbohydrate – starch and fibre (if brown rice)
- B vitamins (thiamin and niacin)
- LBV protein.

Figure 6.2 Crossed grain symbol (symbol for gluten-free produce)

Several varieties of rice are sold in supermarkets, including:

- short-grain rice – used in puddings and risottos, as the grains tend to clump together when they are cooked
- long-grain rice – the grains remain separate when they are cooked. Examples are Carolina rice and basmati.

It is also possible to buy rice as a pre-cooked/prepared product, for example:

- frozen
- chilled (pre-cooked)
- canned
- quick/fast-cook rice
- boil in the bag.

 Maize ———————————————————— Revised ☐

The nutrient content of maize is similar to other cereals. It is a good source of vitamin A.

Maize is available in a variety of forms: fresh, frozen and canned. It is also used to make breakfast cereals such as cornflakes.

In its ground form it is a white powder called cornflour. This is often used to thicken liquids and sauces.

Figure 6.3 Maize products

Oats ———————————————————————— Revised ☐

Oats are a good source of carbohydrates (starch and fibre), B vitamins (thiamin, riboflavin and B6), calcium, iron and small amounts of folic acid.

Oats are usually rolled rather than crushed when they are processed. Oats are mainly used in cereal products, e.g. muesli, and in baked products such as flapjacks and biscuits. Oats can be used to make a non-dairy substitute for milk used by people who have an intolerance to lactose, a milk protein allergy and/or an allergy to soya. The Oatly oat drink shown in Figure 6.4 is also low in saturated fat and helps to lower cholesterol as part of a healthy balanced lifestyle.

Barley ——————————————————————— Revised ☐

The main nutrients found in barley are carbohydrates (fibre and starch). It is used in foods as pearl barley, which can be added to stews and casseroles, or as flaked barley, which is added to breakfast cereals.

Figure 6.4 Oat milk

Check your understanding ————————————————————— Tested ☐

1 Describe what is meant by the term 'extraction rate'. (2 marks)
2 Explain what is meant by the term 'staple food'. (2 marks)
3 State the nutrients used to fortify white flour. (4 marks)
4 List **three** ways in which rice can be purchased. (3 marks)
5 Explain how cereals and cereal products can make a valuable contribution to our diet. (4 marks)

LINK TO TEXTBOOK pages 79, 80, 125

7 Fruits and vegetables

Nutrient content
Revised ☐

The nutrient content of fruits and vegetables is similar. The table below shows good sources of fruits and vegetables and their nutrient content.

Nutrient	Fruits	Vegetables
Protein	Insignificant amounts in fruits	Found in pulses and beans Low biological value, except in soya beans, which are HBV (High Biological Value)
Carbohydrate	Found in the form of sucrose and fructose in ripe fruit Fibre is found in the skin and fibrous parts of the fruit	Root vegetables and tubers are the best sources of carbohydrate, in the form of starch Vegetables are a good source of fibre
Vitamin A	Apricots	Carrots, dark green vegetables
Vitamin C	Rich sources: blackcurrants, rosehips Good sources: citrus fruits, strawberries, gooseberries, raspberries, oranges	Rich sources: sprouts, cabbage, green peppers, spinach, watercress Reasonable sources: peas, bean sprouts, potatoes (especially if the skin is eaten)
B Vitamins	Fruits do not contain significant amounts	Pulses provide a good source of thiamine Most vegetables contain some of the B group
Calcium and iron	Fruits do not contain significant amounts	Found in some vegetables, e.g. watercress, cabbage and spinach, but it is not always available to the body

Table 7.1 Nutrient content of fruits and vegetables

Many vitamins are water-soluble and are destroyed by heat.

Fruits
Revised ☐

- There is a large range of fruits, in a variety of flavours, colours, size and texture.
- They are mostly eaten raw, but on some occasions are cooked.

Vegetables
Revised ☐

- A wide variety of vegetables is available for use all through the year.
- You can buy these in a variety of forms, such as fresh, frozen and canned.

Structure of vegetables

- Vegetables are similar to fruit in structure.
- Vegetables also come in a variety of colours.
- We eat different parts of the vegetable plants and this is how they are classified.

examiner tip

When answering questions, name specific vitamins and minerals.

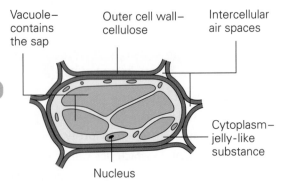

Vacuole – contains the sap
Outer cell wall – cellulose
Intercellular air spaces
Cytoplasm – jelly-like substance
Nucleus

Figure 7.1 Structure of fruit

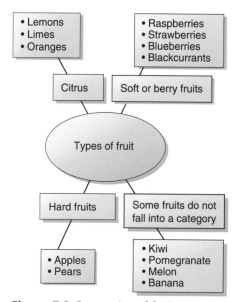

Figure 7.2 Categories of fruits

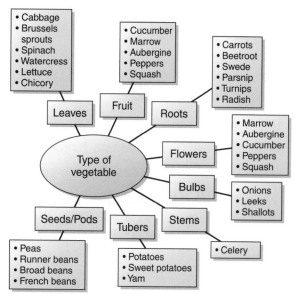

Figure 7.3 Categories of vegetables

Fruits and vegetables need to be carefully prepared to maintain their nutritional profile. They must be stored correctly before they are prepared to help retain their nutritional value. This can be done by:

- storing in a cool, dry place
- handling carefully – bruising will reduce the vitamin C content
- removing any damaged fruit or vegetables
- checking the storage instructions
- keeping salad ingredients in the salad drawer.

When preparing fruits and vegetables:

- Wash to remove dirt.
- Remove any blemishes or outer leaves.
- Peel if necessary.
- Prepare vegetables just before cooking to prevent loss of vitamins by the action of enzymes and oxidization.
- Do not soak them in water, to prevent the loss of water-soluble vitamins.
- Handle delicate fruits and vegetables carefully so they do not get bruised.

Some fruits and vegetables will go brown once they are peeled and cut, e.g. apples, potatoes and pears. This is called enzymic browning.

Check your understanding — Tested

1 State **two** fruits and **two** vegetables that are a good source of vitamin C. (4 marks)
2 State **three** ways you can buy fruits and vegetables. (3 marks)
3 Explain how vegetables should be prepared and cooked to maintain the vitamin C content. (4 marks)
4 Give **three** reasons why we should include more vegetables in our diet. (3 marks)
5 State **three** vegetables that provide protein. (2 marks)

8 Meat and fish

Classification, structure and nutritional value of meat
Revised

Classification of meat

The general term 'meat' is used to refer to meat, game, poultry and offal.

Meat	Game	Poultry	Offal (internal organs of animals)
• Bacon • Beef • Lamb • Mutton • Pork	• Pheasant • Rabbit • Venison	• Chicken • Duck • Goose • Turkey	• Heart • Kidneys • Liver • Tongue • Tripe

Table 8.1 Types of meat

The structure of meat

Meat is the muscle tissue of animals.

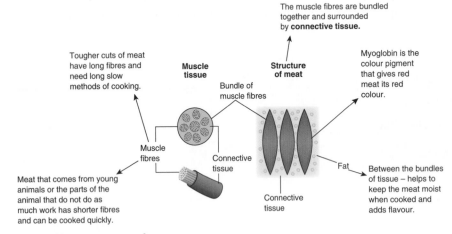

Figure 8.1 Structure of meat

Nutritional value

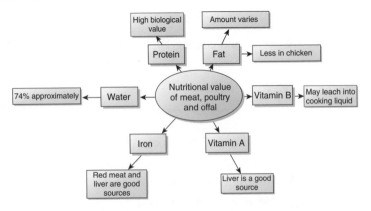

Figure 8.2 Nutritional value of meat, poultry and offal

Preparation of meat
Revised

Meat must be processed, stored, handled and cooked correctly so that it is safe to eat. It is classed as a high-risk food because it contains protein and is moist.

The following is good practice:
● Wash your hands before and after touching any type of raw meat.

- Keep raw meat separate from other foods – cover and store the meat at the bottom of the fridge so that it cannot touch any other foods.
- Raw meat contains harmful bacteria that can spread to anything it touches, so it is important to clean surfaces and equipment thoroughly after preparing meat.
- Raw meat should be stored at temperatures below 5°C.
- Any bacteria present in the meat will be destroyed by heat. It is therefore important to check that the meat is thoroughly cooked. This can be done with a food probe or meat thermometer.

Classification, structure and nutritional value of fish   Revised

There are many varieties of fish available and it is available in many different forms, e.g. fresh, frozen and canned. The government advises that we should eat two portions of fish a week and one of these should be an oily fish.

Classification of fish

Fish can be classified by habitat (sea or freshwater), fat content or type (white, oily or shellfish).
Types of fish include white fish (cod, haddock, coley, whiting, plaice), oily fish (sardines, tuna, mackerel, sardines, trout, salmon) and shellfish (prawns, crab, lobster, shrimps, oysters).

Structure of fish

Fish is made up of fibres and connective tissue. The fibres are much shorter and the connective tissue is much finer, therefore it does not take long to cook.

Nutritional value of fish

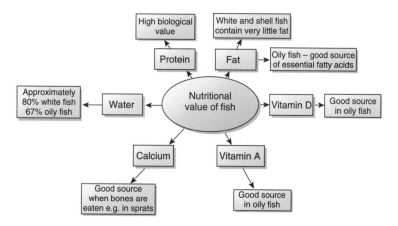

Figure 8.3 Nutritional value of fish

Preparation of fish   Revised

Fresh fish is usually sold as whole fish, or cut into steaks or fillets. When choosing fresh fish, check that it has a sea-fresh smell, the flesh is moist and firm, and the scales are shiny.

Fish is a high-risk food, therefore the same good practice used when preparing meat needs to be applied when preparing fish. It is also wise to wrap fish thoroughly, so that the smell does not pass to other foods.

examiner tip

When a question asks you to explain your answer you must make a statement and then expand on the point.

Check your understanding   Tested

1 Explain why fish takes less time to cook than meat. (2 marks)
2 Explain why it is important to store raw meat and fish away from other foods. (4 marks)
3 State the main nutrients found in red meat. (6 marks)
4 Explain why we are being encouraged to eat at least two portions of fish a week. (4 marks)
5 Describe how would you store fresh meat and fish in the home. (3 marks)

9 Dairy products and eggs

Structure and nutritional value of milk
Revised

Cow's milk is the most popular milk consumed in the UK. Other sources of milk are goats and sheep. There are also milk-type products made from oats, rice or soya, which are lactose free.

Milk is mainly water. It is an **emulsion** and has tiny drops of fat suspended in it. Today much of the milk we buy is **homogenised** and therefore the fat line is not visible.

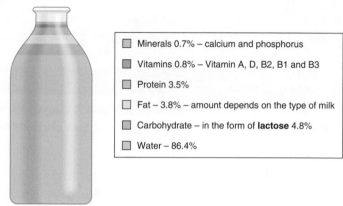

- [ ] Minerals 0.7% – calcium and phosphorus
- [ ] Vitamins 0.8% – Vitamin A, D, B2, B1 and B3
- [ ] Protein 3.5%
- [ ] Fat – 3.8% – amount depends on the type of milk
- [ ] Carbohydrate – in the form of **lactose** 4.8%
- [ ] Water – 86.4%

Figure 9.1 Average nutritional content of milk

Varieties of milk
Revised

- Whole milk has had nothing added or removed – fat content 4 per cent.
- Semi-skimmed milk 1.7 per cent fat.
- Skimmed milk 0.1–0.3 per cent fat.
- Channel Island milk 5.7 per cent fat.

Milk can be processed to produce other types of milk, e.g.

- dried milk powder
- condensed and evaporated milk.

It can also be made into other products such as yoghurt, cream and cheese.

Alternatives to animal milk

Some people have problems digesting cow's milk, as they are allergic to milk, or **lactose** intolerant. They may use an alternative that gives them similar nutrition. Examples include:

- rice milk
- oat milk
- soya milk.

Heat treatment of milk

Most milk is heat treated to kill harmful bacteria and to increase its shelf life. See Chapter 21 for how milk is pasteurised, sterilised and UHT treated.

Structure and nutritional value of cheese
Revised

- There are many different varieties of cheese, made in the UK and in many other countries around the world.
- The flavour, texture and colour of cheese depends on the type of milk it contains (cow, goat, sheep) or the method used to make it.

Structure of cheese

Cheese is made from milk. To change it from a liquid to a solid, rennin (an enzyme, also known as chymosin) is added to the milk. The curd is used to make the cheese. The cheese is then pressed. The harder it is pressed, the less water it contains.

In vegetarian cheese, vegetable rennet is added to the milk in place of rennin.

Nutrients found in cheese

Nutrients in cheese include:

- protein
- calcium
- vitamin A
- riboflavin (vitamin B2)
- fat.

Harder varieties and cream cheeses have a high fat content. Many reduced-fat varieties are available.

Structure and nutritional value of eggs   Revised

Most of the eggs we use come from hens. Duck, goose and quail eggs are also eaten in the UK.

Structure of eggs

Eggs are made up of three main parts:

- shell – the colour of the shell does not affect the nutritional value of the egg
- egg white – there are two parts to the egg white, the thick and thin
- egg yolk – the colour of the yolk is related to what the hens are fed on. The yolk contains **lecithin**.

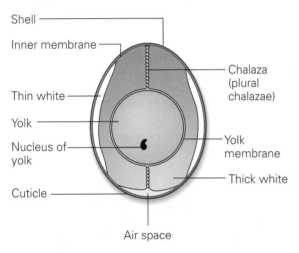

Figure 9.2 Structure of an egg

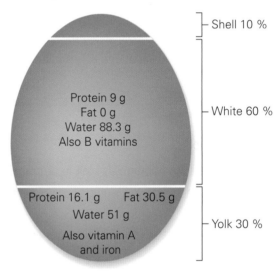

Figure 9.3 Nutrients in eggs

Eggs have a wide variety of uses in food preparation. See Chapter 15 for information about how eggs are used in food preparation.

Check your understanding   Tested

1 State **three** ways the shelf life of milk can be extended. (3 marks)
2 More people are choosing to buy skimmed and semi skimmed milk. Explain why. (2 marks)
3 State **three** nutrients found in cheese. (3 marks)
4 Explain why eggs are an important food in our diet. (4 marks)
5 Explain where you would store eggs, milk and cheese in your home. (2 marks)

10 Fats and oils 2

There are many varieties of fats and oils, and the market is continuing to expand. Fats and oils have many different uses in food preparation.

Sources and nutritional value of fats and oils
Revised

Sources of fats and oils

- Fats and oils can come from both animal and vegetable sources.
- Oils are liquid and fats are solid.
- Oils come from vegetables sources such as olives, corn, rape, nuts, soya, ground nuts and from fish.
- Fats are usually from animal sources.
- The more saturated fatty acids a product has, the more solid the fat will be.
- Animal fats contain more saturated fats than vegetable and fish oils.

Nutrients found in fats

- The main nutrient in fats is fat. However, the amount of different types of fat they contain varies.
- Fats also contain fat-soluble vitamins.
- Vitamin A and D are added to margarine, by law.

Types of fats
Revised

examiner's tip
Butter is available in reduced-fat versions, not low-fat.

Animal fats

- Animal fats are traditionally high in saturated fats.
- Butter is made from milk, animal suet from cattle and lard from pig fat.
- Today, manufacturers make lighter varieties of butter by adding ingredients such as water and vegetable oil.

Margarine

- By law, margarine must have vitamins A and D added to it.
- It must not contain more than 16 per cent water.
- It can be made from either a mixture of animal and vegetable fats and oils or all vegetable oil.
- Some margarines are made using **hydrogenated fats**. However, as technology develops, many more margarines are made using emulsifiers. This means fewer hydrogenated fats and trans fats are contained in margarines.

Low-fat spreads

- Low-fat spreads have a lower fat content than butter or margarine.
- The percentage of water in these products is higher.
- Many low-fat spreads are available.
- Often, they cannot be used for cooking, so the labels on these products need to be read carefully.

Figure 10.1 Animal fats

Figure 10.2 Margarine

White fats

- White fats are made from oils and can be used instead of lard.
- They can be used in products such as pastry and for frying. The consistency of the products can vary.
- Some have air added, making them softer and easier to combine in ingredients, for example when rubbing in pastry.

Oils

- Oils contain 100 per cent fat.
- They mostly contain unsaturated fats from vegetable sources.

Figure 10.3 Low-fat spreads

Figure 10.4 White fats

Figure 10.5 Oils

Check your understanding

Tested

1 List the main nutrients found in fats. (2 marks)
2 Explain why many people are choosing to use vegetable fats and oils. (4 marks)
3 State **two** examples of vegetable oils and **two** examples of animal fats. (4 marks)
4 Explain why some low-fat spreads are not suitable for cooking. (2 marks)
5 State which type of fat has to have vitamins added to it, by law. (1 mark)

11 Alternative protein foods

Types of alternative protein foods

Alternative protein foods provide protein from sources other than animals. A variety of meat-like products are available in supermarkets. They have been developed to resemble meat products.

Soya beans

- Are made into a variety of products including milk, soy sauce and tofu.
- Textured vegetable protein (TVP) is made from soya beans. The mixture is then made into a variety of shapes.
- TVP products can be bought as a canned, dried or frozen product.
- TVP is very bland and needs ingredients with strong flavours to be added to it to make it into an interesting product.

Tofu

- Tofu is made from ground soya beans.
- It is a solid curd and looks like a soft cheese.
- As it is soft, it absorbs flavours.
- It is usually sold from the chiller cabinet.
- It can be frozen, but must be cooked after defrosting.
- It can be grilled or stir-fried.

Tofu —

Shaped TVP —

Soya beans —

Figure 11.1 Soya products

Mycoprotein (Quorn®)

- Mycoprotein is produced from micro-organisms.
- When it is made into a food product it has egg white added to it to bind it together – therefore it is not suitable for vegans.
- It is moulded into a variety of shapes, such as mince, slices and fillets.
- It is also mixed with other ingredients to make ready-to-use products, such as sausages.
- These products are sold from either the chiller cabinet or the freezer.

> **examiner's tip**
> Remember that Quorn® is not suitable for vegans as it contains egg white.

Alternative protein foods are low in fat. They contain the following nutrients:

● **protein** – soya beans are **high biological value (HBV) proteins**

● **vitamins** and minerals – alternative protein foods have often been enriched with these, e.g. soya **fortified** with B12.

● **fibre**, often found in soya mince and Quorn®.

Preparation of alternative protein foods — Revised

● Ready meals made using alternative protein foods must be reheated in a microwave or oven.

● Products such as Quorn® mince need other ingredients added to provide colour and flavour.

● The cooking instructions must be followed carefully for all these products.

● When preparing and cooking alternative protein foods as cook-chill products, treat them as high-risk foods.

Figure 11.2 Quorn® products

Check your understanding — Tested

1 Explain why mycoprotein (Quorn®) is not suitable for vegans. (2 marks)

2 Explain why soya products are important for people who follow a vegan diet. (2 marks)

3 State **two** products that can be made from soya beans. (2 marks)

4 Soya beans do not have a lot of flavour. State **three** ingredients you could use with the soya to give it more flavour. (3 marks)

5 State **two** alternative protein products that contain all the essential amino acids. (2 marks)

Diet and food choice

12 Diet and food choice

There are many factors to consider when choosing foods to provide a balanced diet.

Ages and stages of life — Revised ☐

Babies are totally dependent on parents to provide food. Milk is the ideal food for this stage.

Toddlers grow fast and require a lot of energy. They need:

- **complex carbohydrates** as they are the best source of energy
- to be encouraged to try new foods
- to develop independence, so should be allowed to hold their food and learn to feed themselves.

Teenagers need food to be:

- affordable, fashionable, quick and easy to prepare
- full of energy from complex carbohydrates
- rich in iron for girls, high in carbohydrates for boys
- rich in calcium and phosphorus.

Senior citizens:

- may be on a low income
- may have loss of appetite so food needs to be appealing
- may need smaller quantities
- need easy to open packaging
- need easy to prepare foods.

Figure 12.1 Babies

Figure 12.2 Toddlers

Figure 12.3 Teenagers

Other factors to consider when choosing foods — Revised ☐

Other factors include:

- availability – a wide variety is available, due to technological developments
- cost – save money by buying special offers/buying short shelf life/ using cheaper proteins

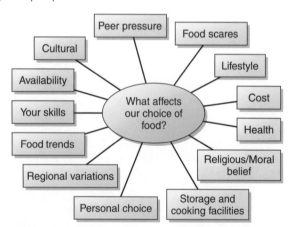

Peer pressure

Cultural

Availability

Your skills

Food trends

Regional variations

Personal choice

Food scares

Lifestyle

Cost

Health

Religious/Moral belief

Storage and cooking facilities

What affects our choice of food?

Figure 12.5 Factors affecting food choice

Figure 12.4 Adults

Figure 12.6 Senior citizens

- personal preference – we are influenced by sight, sound, smell, taste, touch (known as **organoleptic** qualities)
- cultural preferences – eating patterns vary, according to beliefs, values, where we live and foods available
- religious issues – religions often have food laws
- moral issues – some people think that it is morally wrong to kill animals, to factory farm and/or use **GM** crops. They may choose to buy **fair-trade** and/or **organic**, products, and/or to use local or seasonal foods.
- lifestyle – demand for food that is easy to prepare (e.g. simple recipes, ready-meals)
- health – making changes to improve our health
- storage and cooking – facilities may be limited
- food scares – reports in the media may cause people to stop eating certain foods
- advertising and promotions – we may be persuaded to buy certain products.

Vegetarians
Revised

There are three main reasons why a person might become vegetarian:
- moral reasons
- religious beliefs
- medical reasons.

Lacto-ovo vegetarians

- **Lacto-ovo vegetarians** will not eat anything that involves killing an animal.
- Will not eat meat, meat products, fish, poultry, lard, suet, fish oils or gelatine.
- They will eat food products from animals such as eggs, milk, cheese, butter, cream and yoghurt.
- They have no problem at all in obtaining the essential amino acids for proteins or a wide range of vitamins and minerals.

Figure 12.7 Look out for the vegetarian logo

Vegans
Revised

- **Vegans** avoid eating all animal products: meat, fish, eggs, cheese, dairy milk and cream. They eat nuts and nut products, pulses, cereals, vegetables and fruits.
- They must ensure that they have a nutritionally balanced diet, in particular an adequate supply of:
  - proteins, to ensure that they get all the essential amino acids
  - vitamin D, which the body can manufacture from exposure to sun, but may need to be supplemented if sun exposure is not possible
  - calcium, phosphorus and iron
  - vitamin B12, as there is no B12 in cereals or vegetables.

> **examiner tip**
>
> Remember not to include **mycoprotein** (Quorn®) in meals for vegans, as it contains egg white.

Check your understanding
Tested

1 State **four** reasons why a person may become a vegetarian. (4 marks)
2 Explain the difference between a vegan and a lacto-ovo vegetarian. (2 marks)
3 Name **three** protein foods that would be suitable for use in a main course product for vegans. (3 marks)
4 Give **four** factors that affect a teenager's choice of food. (4 marks)
5 The sales of ready meals have risen in recent years. Give **three** reasons for this increase. (3 marks)

13 Special diets

Coronary heart disease (CHD) — Revised ☐

- Risk of heart disease is increased by smoking, high blood pressure, high cholesterol, obesity, family history, inadequate exercise.
- The development of coronary heart disease is linked to the amount of fat in the diet.
- A diet high in saturated fats is likely to be high in cholesterol.
- **Cholesterol** is a substance made in the liver and carried in the bloodstream. It can build up and be deposited with other material on the walls of the arteries.
- Blocked arteries cause a person to have a heart attack, which can cause death.

examiner tip
Do not mix up the terms 'heart attack' and 'coronary heart disease'.

Figure 13.1 Individuals have differing dietary needs

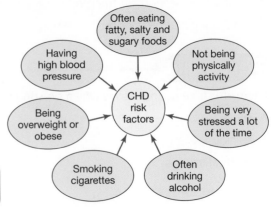

Figure 13.2 CHD risk factors

People with diabetes — Revised ☐

- **Diabetes** is a medical condition where the glucose in the blood stream is not balanced correctly.
- Glucose is carried by blood to all body cells to supply them with energy.
- Insulin, a hormone produced by the pancreas, controls the amount of glucose in the bloodstream and stops it going too high.
- Meals for diabetics should include high-fibre, starchy carbohydrate foods, but should be low in sugar and sweet foods.

Figure 13.3 Diabetes risk factors

Pregnant women — Revised ☐

During pregnancy, a woman does not need special food products but must ensure that she has a varied, balanced diet. She must make sure that she has an adequate supply of the following:

- protein, for the growth of the baby
- calcium and vitamin D, for her own and for the baby's bone and tooth development
- folic acid, to make new cells in the developing baby (should be taken in supplements before and during the early stages of pregnancy)
- iron, as the developing baby needs it for its blood supply
- a good supply of fruit and vegetables to provide vitamin C and fibre
- not too many fats and sugary foods, so that she does not put on too much weight.

Food allergies and intolerances

Revised

- Some people cannot eat certain types of food without becoming ill. They may have a food intolerance or food allergy. Allergic reactions are sometimes severe.
- In an allergic reaction, the body reacts strongly to a particular substance. Common allergens include eggs, soya and nuts. Some artificial food flavours, colours or preservatives can also cause reactions.

Nut allergy

- The allergic reaction to nuts is very serious.
- Some people have an **anaphylactic reaction** to even a minute quantity of an allergen in nuts.
- The possibility of even the smallest amount of nut contact during food production must be noted on the product label.

Coeliac disease

- **Coeliac disease** is caused by a reaction to the protein **gluten**.
- Gluten is found in cereals, especially wheat. Also in barley, rye and oats.
- The gluten damages the lining of the intestine and prevents other nutrients from being absorbed.
- Food manufactures use it as a thickening, so people with coeliac disease must read ingredient lists carefully.
- Gluten-free products are available.

Figure 13.4 Crossed grain symbol (for gluten-free produce)

Lactose intolerance

- A person with lactose intolerance cannot digest the milk sugar lactose.
- Symptoms are abdominal pain and diarrhoea.
- They have to avoid dairy milk and milk products.

Food intolerances are increasing and products have to list their ingredients on their packaging by law.

> **examiner tip**
>
> Check the latest list of allergens/intolerances on the Food Standards website before your examination.

Check your understanding

Tested

1 Give **four** changes that a person with heart disease should make to their diet. (4 marks)
2 List **four** risk factors that cause people to have CHD. (4 marks)
3 State **four** starchy foods that a person with coeliac disease could eat instead of bread. (4 marks)
4 Name **one** product that a lactose intolerance sufferer could use instead of dairy milk. (1 mark)
5 Explain why it is important for a pregnant mother to have calcium and iron. (2 marks)

14 Energy balance

The Department of Health has put together data advising people of the quantities of different nutrients and energy from food needed by various groups. This list gives dietary reference values (DRVs). This is a list of estimates of the amount of energy and nutrients needed by different groups of people in the UK population.

Figure 14.1 Stages of life

Dietary reference values
Revised

Included in this are:

- **RNI (reference nutrient intake)**, which shows the estimated quantities needed for 97 per cent of the population. These are too high for many individuals.
- **EAR (estimated average requirements)**, which gives an average estimate of amounts, so some people will need more and others less.
- **LRNI (lower reference nutrient intake)** is the amount of a nutrient that is enough for only a small number of people who have low needs.

The relationship between food intake and physical activity
Revised

This is known as **energy balance**. Energy is measured in **kilocalories (kcal) or kilojoules (kJ)**. Carbohydrates, fats and protein from all the food and drinks we consume are broken down in the digestive system and contribute to the total daily amount of our energy:
The amount of energy we need varies according to:

- age
- gender
- how much energy is used for all bodily functions (breathing, warmth, nerves, digestion, brain function), referred to as our **basal metabolic rate (BMR)**
- the amount of activity carried out
- occupation
- the time of year
- state of health.

> **examiner tip**
>
> Energy balance is often used as a 6-mark banded question. Make sure that you can explain about each of these factors.

Balancing energy

It is important to balance the amount of energy consumed in foods with the amount of energy used.

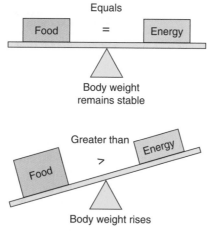

Figure 14.2 It is all a matter of balance

- If food consumed equals the energy used, body weight stays the same.
- If food consumed is greater than energy used, it is stored as fat and weight increases.
- If food consumed is less than energy used, there is weight loss.

Obesity

- The number of people who are overweight or obese is increasing in the UK.
- Being overweight is unhealthy because it puts a strain on the organs of the body.
- In general, people are doing less exercise but eating the same amount of food.
- Obesity can cause heart disease, high blood pressure, diabetes, osteoarthritis, varicose veins, breathlessness and chest infections.
- It may also cause low self-esteem and may lead to depression.

Losing weight

- The only way to lose weight is to reduce the number of calories consumed and combine this with increased physical exercise.
- Meals for people who are trying to lose weight should include a variety of foods and follow the Eatwell Plate, reducing their intake of fat and sugar.
- People trying to lose weight should use low-fat methods of cooking such as grilling, steaming, boiling and stir-frying.

Check your understanding

Tested

1 State what is meant by the term 'energy balance'. (2 marks)
2 Explain why the UK Government gives DRVs (dietary reference values). (2 marks)
3 Explain how we can increase the energy used by our body. (1 mark)
4 Describe what happens to any Kcals we eat that are additional to our requirements. (1 mark)
5 List **five** factors that affect the amount of energy our body needs. (5 marks)

15 Functions of ingredients

Ingredient	Function	Example
Flour	Forms main structure of a product, due to its gluten content Bulking Raising agent if self-raising flour is used Thickens (gelatinisation)	Bread: strong plain flour – high gluten content Cakes: soft plain flour – low gluten content to give a soft, tender crumb Crumble: topping; Pastry: casing Cakes Sauces
Fat Oils	Adds colour and flavour if butter or margarine is used Holds air bubbles during mixing to create texture and volume Helps extend shelf life Shortens a flour mixture to make a crisp or crumbly texture Shortening Frying/sautéing Forming emulsions Binds ingredients together	Cakes, biscuits Cakes, biscuits, pastry Pastry Pastry Biscuits and pastry Stir-fry Salad dressing
Eggs	Add colour and flavour Hold air when whisked Form an emulsion when mixed with fat Bind ingredients together Coagulating/setting Glazing Coating/enrobing Enriching – thickening Gives a smooth glossy finish Adding nutritional value	Cakes Meringue, whisked sponge Mayonnaise Beefburgers, fish cakes Quiche Lorraine Pastry Holding dry coatings (e.g. breadcrumbs) onto a surface and forming a barrier during cooking processes (e.g. fried, breaded fish) Sauces Choux pastry
Sugar	Sweetens Develops flavour Increases bulk of the mixture Holds air when creamed with fat Aids fermentation Preserves	Desserts, cakes Soft brown sugar, or treacle in a gingerbread Cakes Victoria sandwich Bread Jam
Liquid	Acts as a raising agent when converted to steam Binds ingredients together Glazing (milk) Enrich (milk)	Cakes, batters Pastry Scones Bread
Salt	Helps develop flavour Strengthens gluten in flour and controls action of yeast Preserves	Pastry Breads Fish
Baking Powder	Aerates	Makes cake rise
Yeast	Aerates	Makes bread rise
Fruit and Vegetables	Adds colour and flavour Adds texture Thickens Adds nutritional value Garnish To add as a topping	Savoury and sweet dishes Savoury and sweet dishes When cooked and pureed e.g. soups, sauces Tomato Potato on shepherds pie
Herbs and spices	Improve and add flavour Garnish	Curry, Chilli Parsley

continued on next page

Continued

Ingredient	Function	Example
Gelatine	Setting	Jelly, Chilled desserts e.g. cheesecakes, souffle
Chocolate, Icings	Coats or decorates	Biscuits, cakes, desserts

Table 15.1 Functions of ingredients

Raising agents
Revised

Raising agents are added to a cake, bread mixture, etc. to give lightness to the mixture. Raising agents include:

- air
- carbon dioxide
- water vapour or steam.

Air can be added by:

- sieving flour
- rubbing fat into flour
- creaming fat and sugar together
- beating mixtures, e.g. batters
- folding and rolling, e.g. flaky pastry
- whisking.

Carbon dioxide can be introduced by the use of:

- bicarbonate of soda plus acid, e.g. cream of tartar
- baking powder.

Self-raising flour is a prepared mixture of a soft (plain) flour and a raising agent.
When given food, warmth, moisture and time, yeast produces carbon dioxide by the process of fermentation.
Water vapour or steam is produced during cooking from liquids in the mixture.

examiner tip

You must state the correct function of an ingredient for the food product you are being asked about.

Figure 15.1 Whisking eggs and sugar

Figure 15.2 Yeast causes dough to rise

Check your understanding
Tested

1 The following ingredients are required to make a lemon meringue pie. State the function of each ingredient.
    pastry base – flour, fat, water
        filling and topping – lemon, eggs, cornflour, sugar.   (7 marks)
2 State **one** function of the following ingredients used in bread making.
  a) yeast
  b) strong plain flour.   (2 marks)
3 State **two** conditions necessary for yeast to function correctly.   (2 marks)
4 A manufacturer wants to develop a new biscuit from the following ingredients: 50 g margarine, 50 g caster sugar, ½ an egg, 100 g self-raising flour.
  a) Suggest **two** flavourings that could be added to the biscuit mixture. (2 marks)
  b) Suggest **one** ingredient that could be added to the biscuit mixture to change the texture. (1 mark)
  c) Give **one** function of the sugar in the biscuit mixture. (1 mark)

Additives and food components

16 Additives and food components

Additives

Additives are substances that are added to foods during manufacturing or processing to improve quality and keep costs down.

Why additives are used

Additives are used to:

- improve keeping qualities
- improve colour, flavour, texture and appearance
- help keep the price of food competitive
- give an improved **nutritional profile**.

All additives are checked for safety. When they are passed, they are given a number. Many additives are artificial, i.e. made from chemicals or synthetic compounds. However, many people prefer foods containing additives from natural sources, e.g. red colouring from beetroot.

Advantages and disadvantages

During manufacturing, additives:

- can be used in a wide range of products
- improve specific characteristics
- produce expected qualities
- allow a product range, e.g. flavoured crisps
- maintain product consistency in large-scale production
- restore original characteristics after processing food
- prevent spoilage and give a longer shelf life
- disguise inferior ingredients, so reducing costs.

Disadvantages to the consumer:

- Some people may have an allergy to additives.
- Some people object to having artificial ingredients and chemicals added to their food.

Types	Function
Colours	To make food attractive: to replace colour lost during heat treatment (e.g. canned peas); to boost colour, e.g. strawberry yoghurt
Preservatives	To keep food safe for longer. Extending shelf life, reduces number of shopping trips; prevents growth of micro-organisms causing food spoilage
Sweeteners	Two types: Intense – in low-calorie drinks and reduced sugar products. Lack the bulk needed for cooking. Bulk – use in small amounts. In sugar-free confectionary, preserves for diabetics
Emulsifiers, stabilisers	Improve consistency during processing and storage. Ingredients when mixed do not separate e.g. salad cream
Flavourings and flavour enhancers	Make existing flavour stronger. Replace flavour lost during processing
Antioxidants	Help prevent foods containing fats and oils becoming rancid. Prevents some foods from becoming brown

Table 16.1 Types of additives and their function

Fortification

Some foods have nutrients added to increase their nutritional value. Manufacturers sometimes see fortification as an advantage to sell more products. Reasons for fortification include:

- to increase nutritional content
- to help reduce nutrition deficiencies
- to replace nutrients lost during processing

Figure 16.1 Fortified foods

Examples of foods fortified by law include: bread (iron, vitamin B/ folic acid, calcium, omega 3 oil); margarine and butter (vitamins A and D).

Examples of voluntary fortification include: fruit juice (vitamin C); low-fat spreads (vitamins A and D).

examiner tip

It is important that in your answer you state that fortification increases the nutritional value.

Food components

Revised

Components are individual parts that make up a product.

Standard components	Pre-manufactured components
Concentrate, e.g. tomato puree	Ready-made pastry
Stock cubes	Pre-washed and pre-prepared vegetables
Flavourings, e.g. vanilla essence	Ready-to-roll icing
Herbs and spices	Crumble mix

Table 16.2 Standard and pre-manufactured components

Advantages/benefits	Disadvantages/limitations
Save preparation time	Rely upon a manufacturer to supply the product – their problems become yours
Saves staff skill, costs and equipment	Taste and quality may be inferior to using your own ingredients
Results are the same every time	Other food companies may use the same components
Quality is guaranteed	May be expensive
Components come from experts who know how to make them	May contain ingredients that the consumer wishes to avoid, e.g. artificial colourants
Some have a relatively long shelf life	May contain added fat, sugar or salt
Can be used as part of more complex products	Could have poor proportions, e.g. little meat compared to sauce
Saves relying on several suppliers to provide the separate ingredients	

Table 16.3 Advantages and disadvantages of pre-manufactured components

examiner tip

Make sure you read the question carefully. Does it ask for the benefits to the manufacturer or to the consumer?

Check your understanding

Tested

1 State the function in food products of:

a) Preservatives

b) Antioxidants

c) Emulsifiers and stabilisers. (3 marks)

2 Give **four** advantages to the manufacturer of using additives. (4 marks)

3 Give **one** reason some people choose to purchase foods that do not contain additives. (1 mark)

4 Explain what is meant by 'fortification'. (2 marks)

5 Give **two** reasons why a manufacturer would buy ready-made icing and decorations as pre-manufactured components. (2 marks)

17 Methods of cooking and heat transference

Heat transference

There are three ways in which heat is transferred: conduction, radiation and convection.

Conduction (Boiling, baking, frying, microwaving, roasting)	Radiation (BBQ, grilling, microwaving)	Convection (Baking, boiling, frying, roasting, steaming)
Heat is transferred by contact with heat.	Direct rays pass from the heat source to the food.	Heat moves through the convection currents.

Table 17.1 Methods of heat transference

Moist methods of cooking

Method	Advantages	Disadvantages
Boiling (uses large amounts of rapidly bubbling liquid to cook foods)	Quick, food is not likely to burn, simple	Food may disintegrate, water-soluble vitamins may be lost, flavour from foods may leach into water
Simmering (foods cooked in hot liquid (85–99°C))	Can be used for foods requiring gentler treatment than boiling	
Poaching (temperature of the liquid just below simmering)	Foods do not need a long cooking time	
Steaming (food does not come into contact with water – cooked by steam)	Loss of water-soluble nutrients reduced, food is light in texture, different foods cooked in different tiers to reduce energy costs	Some products can take a long time to cook, delicate foods easily overcooked (e.g. fish)

Table 17.2 Moist methods of cooking

Dry methods of cooking

> **examiner tip**
> Remember that cooking several vegetables at once reduces energy consumption.

Baking

- When food is baked it uses mainly dry heat.
- Moisture may be added to help develop certain textures in a food.
- The temperature used varies depending on the type of food product being cooked.
- Baking is regarded as a healthy way of cooking, as fat is not usually involved.

Grilling

Advantages:

- Grilling is a quick method of cooking.
- Often, adding fat is not necessary.
- It reduces the fat content of some foods, e.g. sausages.

Disadvantages:

- Grilling is not suitable for tough cuts of meat.
- Careful timing of cooking is needed so that foods are not overcooked.

Roasting

- A small amount of fat is also used to prevent the food drying out and to develop flavour.
- Roasted foods include vegetables and meat.

Frying

Dry	Shallow	Deep	Stir fry
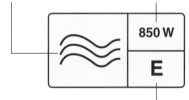			
No fat added.	Fat comes about half way up the food.	Food is totally covered in fat during the frying process.	Relatively healthy method of cooking food as very little fat or oil is used.

Table 17.3 The four types of frying

Advantages:

- Frying is a quick method of cooking.
- Fried food is attractive in colour.
- Soluble nutrients are not lost.

Disadvantages:

- Heat-sensitive nutrients are destroyed.
- We need to limit the amount of fat we eat.
- Fried food is more difficult to digest.

Microwaving

Microwave ovens work by the microwaves entering the food and causing the molecules of water in the food to vibrate. The friction produces the heat.
Microwave ovens should be labelled.

The microwave symbol i.e. three lines of waves, one above the other

The power output in watts, e.g. 850 W. The higher the wattage, the quicker it cooks

850 W

E

The heating category of the oven i.e. a letter from 'A' to 'E'. This is a graded rating to show the oven's ability to heat small food packs e.g. a ready-made meal. A category 'A' oven takes longer than a category 'E'

Figure 17.1 Microwave oven label

Advantages:

- Microwaves save energy.
- They are useful for people who have busy lifestyles.
- There is less destruction of heat-sensitive nutrients.
- There is only a small loss of water-soluble vitamins.
- The bright colour of vegetables is retained.
- They are useful for defrosting frozen food.

Disadvantages:

- Foods can easily be overcooked.
- Flavours may not develop in the food.
- The colour of the food may be pale and therefore not very attractive.

Check your understanding

Tested

1 Explain why stir-frying is considered a healthy method of cooking. (2 marks)
2 We are being encouraged to reduce the amount of energy we use when cooking meals. Explain how this can be done in the home. (6 marks)
3 Describe how a microwave cooks food. (3 marks)
4 State the **three** methods of heat transference. (3 marks)
5 Describe the advantages and disadvantages of grilling foods. (4 marks)

18 The effect of heat on different foods

Protein foods
Revised

When moist or dry heat is applied to proteins, the proteins in the foods **coagulate** (set). When proteins are overheated they become tough and more difficult to digest and **synerisis** occurs.

Food	What happens to the food when it is heated
Meat	• The muscle fibres start to coagulate between 40°C and 60°C. • After 60°C the fibres in the meat shrink and the juice is squeezed out. • The fat melts. • The colour changes from red to brown if it is cooked by a dry method. • B vitamins may be leached into the cooking liquid.
Fish	• The muscles shrink. • Some of the B vitamins are lost as they are destroyed by heat.
Eggs	• The egg white begins to coagulate at 60°C. The egg white changes to a white colour. • The egg yolk begins to coagulate at 70°C.
Milk	• A skin develops on its surface.
Cheese	• The fat melts and the proteins coagulate. • Fat emerges onto the surface.

Table 18.1

Starchy foods
Revised

When dry heat is applied to flour products, the crust of the product becomes brown – this is called **dextrinisation**.

When flour is mixed with a liquid as in a sauce, the mixture will thicken. This is known as **gelatinisation**. This occurs because:

● the starch grains are not able to dissolve in the liquid

● as the liquid is heated, the starch grains swell and as more heat is applied, the starch grains break open, causing the mixture to thicken.

Other starch foods that thicken mixtures are:

● potatoes

● other root vegetables

● rice/rice flour

● arrowroot

● cornflour

Food manufacturers use a lot of starches in products. See Chapter 36.

Figure 18.1 Types of thickener

Sugars Revised

When moist heat is used on sugars, the sugar melts and becomes syrup. At 154°C, the sugar starts to change colour – this process is called caramelisation.

When dry heat is used on sugars, the sugar will also caramelise. When sugars are mixed with other products, such as eggs and flour, a Maillard reaction occurs.

Fruits and vegetables Revised

Fruits and vegetables need to be cooked carefully to retain their nutritive value. The following cooking methods help to retain the vitamin C content:

- Cut into small pieces so they cook quickly.
- Add to boiling water, or steam them.
- Use as little water as possible.
- Cook for as little time as possible.
- Serve them immediately.

Some vegetables (e.g. potatoes) are cooked to make them more digestible.

When fruits and vegetables are cooked they may also change in colour. If green vegetables are overcooked, the colour fades, making them less appealing to the consumer.

Figure 18.2 Crème brûlée

Figure 18.3 Maillard reaction

> **examiner tip**
>
> When answering questions about a nutrient, remember to name it

Check your understanding Tested

1 Describe what happens to proteins when they are heated. (2 marks)
2 Explain what happens to the ingredients in a sauce when they are cooked. (3 marks)
3 State why potatoes need to be cooked. (1 mark)
4 Describe what happens to sugars when moist heat is applied. (2 marks)
5 State **three** ways in which you can reduce the loss of vitamin C when cooking vegetables. (3 marks)

19 Tools and equipment

Using tools and equipment
Revised ☐

The correct equipment must be chosen in order to:

- complete tasks safely, hygienically and efficiently
- achieve a consistency of finish
- achieve a quality outcome.

Job	Equipment
Measuring ingredients	Scales, jugs, spoons
Cutting and chopping a range of foods • Raw meat • Raw fish • Cooked meat • Salad and fruit • Bakery and dairy • Vegetables Grating cheese, vegetables	Processor Knives and chopping boards – different colours for different jobs: • Red • Blue • Yellow • Green • White • Brown Grater
Whisking air into mixtures, e.g. fatless sponge	Hand whisks – balloon, wire or rotary Electric mixer – hand or free standing
Spreading and lifting	Spatula, fish slice, palette knife
Aerating flour, separating solids from liquids	Sieve
Mixing: – rubbing fat into flour – kneading bread dough	Food processor Large food mixer
Puréeing fruit and vegetables	Sieve, blender, smoothie maker

Table 19.1 The right equipment for the job

Large-scale equipment
Revised ☐

- Large-scale equipment used in industry is different to equipment used in the domestic setting.
- People using the equipment have to be properly trained.
- Machines can perform repetitive tasks efficiently, accurately, safely and with a consistency of outcome.
- Machines can save time and effort.
- Equipment selected for industrial use must conform to European Union safety directives.
- Equipment must carry the CE mark, which indicates the required safety standards have been met.

> **examiner tip**
>
> Think about all the practical work that you have done for your controlled assessment. Use this experience when you answer the questions.

Manufactured under an ISO 9001 quality system

Conforms to all relevant British and European Standards

Figure 19.1 CE mark

Small-scale equipment	Large-scale equivalent
Balance scales	Computer-controlled scales
Sharp knife and chopping board	Automatic slicer
Peeler	Mechanical peeler
Rolling out with a rolling pin	Dough is sheeted using rollers
Cutting dough with tart cutters	Dough is cut using rollers with blades

continued on next page

Continued

Small-scale equipment	Large-scale equivalent
Cooking in a saucepan	Large bratt pans
Cooking in an oven	Computer controlled travelling or tunnel ovens
Cooling on a wire tray	Blast chilled in cooling tunnels
Portion controlled with a spoon measure	Squeezed out with an extruder
Piping bag for biscuits	A depositing machine would be used

Table 19.2 Small-scale equipment and the large-scale equivalent

Using tools and equipment safely and effectively
Revised

All equipment should be safe, properly maintained and used correctly. Some materials need regular disinfection to kill or reduce micro-organisms.

Use knives correctly to avoid accidents and cross-contamination:

- Do not leave in a bowl of water – someone could cut themselves.
- Use different coloured knives for raw and cooked food, or wash between uses.
- Use a chopping board.
- Pass by the handle.
- Do not use if damaged.
- Keep sharp.
- Store correctly in a knife box.

Electrical equipment
Revised

- Buy from a reputable retailer.
- Keep away from water.
- Check regularly for frayed wires, etc.
- Ensure it is in good working order before using, e.g. no damage.
- Plug in correctly.
- Only one person should operate the equipment.
- Keep hands away from moving parts.
- Wash blades from processors with care.
- Place equipment away from the edge of work surfaces.
- Turn off after use.

Safety rules when using an oven or hob
Revised

- Turn saucepan handles inwards.
- Use oven gloves when removing hot dishes from the oven.
- Do not leave oven door open or the grill unattended.
- Turn off after use.
- Make sure gas is lit when using a gas cooker.
- Reposition oven shelves before heating.
- Use correct size ring for pan.
- Do not clean while still hot.
- Stir hot liquids with wooden spoon – not metal – because metal is a good conductor of heat
- Maintain and service regularly.
- Tie hair back and do not wear loose clothing when cooking – it may catch fire.

Check your understanding
Tested

1 State **two** rules for the safe use of knives. (2 marks)
2 State **two** uses of a food processor. (2 marks)
3 State the colour of the chopping board used to prepare raw fish. (1 mark)
4 Give **one** reason why the correct piece of equipment should be chosen when carrying out a task. (1 mark)
5 Explain what is meant by the CE mark. (2 marks)

Food spoilage and storage

20 Food spoilage and storage

Micro-organisms and enzymes

Revised

Deterioration of food is caused by **micro-organisms** and **enzymes**.

Micro-organisms

- Some foods may contain micro-organisms, e.g. salmonella in chicken. Others are transferred by poor hygiene practices. If foods are described as **contaminated** they are not safe to eat.
- Some micro-organisms are known as **pathogenic bacteria** and are harmful.
- Others perform useful functions in the production of food products, e.g. cheese, yoghurt.

	Function in industry	**Spoilage**	**Conditions need for growth**
Yeast	Bread-making by the process of **fermentation**	High-sugar foods, e.g. jam	Warmth, moisture, food, time
Moulds	Produce specific flavours and textures, e.g. blue-veined cheeses	Thread-like filaments on the surface of food, e.g. bread	Moisture, temperature between 20°C and 30°C They grow slowly in dry, cold conditions
Bacteria	Cheese and yoghurt	Those causing food poisoning are known as pathogenic bacteria	Warmth, moisture, food, oxygen Neutral **pH** conditions Most active between 5°C – 65°C **Optimum** temperature – 37°C. Reproduce very quickly. Dormant below 0°C. Most cannot survive above 70°C

Table 20.1 Micro-organisms

Enzymes

Enzymes are proteins that speed up chemical reactions. They are used in a range of manufacturing processes, e.g. speeding up ripening during cheese making.

Enzymes can cause browning. To prevent this, **blanch** cut vegetables; dip cut fruit in lemon juice.

Figure 20.1 Mould on cheese and cucumber sandwich

High-risk and low-risk foods

Revised

- **High-risk foods** are high in protein and moisture and are easily contaminated by bacteria.
- High-risk foods must be kept refrigerated.
- **Low-risk foods** have a longer shelf life, so are not so easily contaminated by bacteria.

High-risk foods (often have high protein and moisture content)	**Low-risk foods**
- Raw fish - Dairy products - Cooked meat and poultry - Shellfish and seafood - Gravies, sauces, stocks and stews - Egg products, e.g. raw egg in chilled desserts and mayonnaise - Cooked rice	- High acid content, e.g. pickles - High sugar content, e.g. jam - Sugar-based confectionery, e.g. sweets - Unprocessed, raw vegetables

Table 20.2 High-risk and low-risk foods

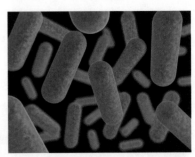

Figure 20.2 E. coli bacteria seen under a microscope

Refrigerator

- Provides safe storage of food, with less risk of contamination.
- Stores food at a temperature of 8°C or below.

Sensible use of your fridge:

- Avoid opening the door regularly to prevent warm air entering.
- Avoid putting in hot food – this fills the inside with steam, which condenses on the shelves and lining, raising the temperature of other foods.
- Cover food.
- Place raw meat/fish on a lower shelf to avoid contamination from 'dripping'.

Freezer

- Stores food at a temperature of −18°C or below.
- A freezer 'star' rating indicates the temperature range of the freezer section in the refrigerator and the length of time you can store foods.
- A freezer that is labelled as shown in Figure 20.3 can be used to freeze fresh foods.
- Frozen foods are transported in temperature-controlled vehicles and immediately placed in freezers at the supermarket.
- Never refreeze food after it has been thawed.
- Foods that contain a large proportion of water and a delicate cell structure do not freeze well. Ice crystals damage the cell structure, causing it to collapse. For example:
  - baked egg custard separates
  - cream separates
  - bananas turn black
  - jelly collapses
  - salad becomes limp.

> **examiner tip**
> Cooked rice is a high-risk food. Uncooked rice is not.

Figure 20.3 Freezer label

Check your understanding   Tested

1 Storing food correctly at home is important. For each of the following foods state (i) where it should be stored; and (ii) why it is stored in this place. For example, dried pasta is stored in a cool, dry place such as a cupboard so moisture does not affect the pasta.
   a) Fresh fruit salad (2 marks)
   b) Ice cream (2 marks)

2 Name **one** high-risk food. (1 mark)

3 Name **one** bacteria that can cause food poisoning. (1 mark)

4 State **one** reason why freezing will prevent bacteria from growing. (1 mark)

5 Explain why cucumbers are not suitable for freezing. (2 marks)

Preservation and extending shelf life

21 Preservation and extending shelf life

Benefits and limitations of preserving food

Benefits:

- prevents **micro-organisms** multiplying and action of enzymes
- increases shelf life – fewer shopping trips
- foods are available when not in season
- increases range of foods available – greater variety
- can save time, effort, fuel and less waste, e.g. ready-meals
- can provide ready-to-use foods that do not require preparation.

Limitations:

- can be expensive
- processed foods are often high in fat, sugar, salt and low in fibre
- some nutrients are lost during processing
- additives are often added to restore colour, flavour and texture
- texture may change, e.g. canned strawberries are very soft.

High-temperature methods of preserving

Pasteurisation

- **Pathogenic** micro-organisms are destroyed (72°C for 15 seconds).
- Shelf life is extended for a limited time.
- Milk and some soups are pasteurised.

Sterilisation

- The product is heated to 104°C for 40 minutes.
- It destroys nearly all micro-organisms and **enzymes**.
- Milk and fruit juices can be sterilised.

Ultra heat treatment (UHT)

- Uses very high temperatures: 130°C for 1–5 seconds.
- It destroys all bacteria.
- Shelf life is extended to six months if the product is not opened.
- There is little colour change, slight change in taste.
- There is little loss of nutrients.
- Sold in airtight cartons.
- Can be used to treat milk, soups and other foods.

Canning

- This is a form of sterilisation. The time and temperature vary depending on the food.
- A huge range of canned foods is available, e.g. soup, vegetables, fruit.
- The texture may change, and there is some loss of nutrients.

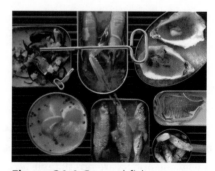

Figure 21.1 Canned fish

> **examiner tip**
> Make sure you know about these methods. You may get a question about milk in the exam.

Low-temperature methods of preserving

This slows down bacterial growth but does not destroy the bacteria – they become dormant. As food warms, bacteria start to reproduce.

Chilling

- Suitable for perishable foods, e.g. prepared salads, sandwiches.
- Foods have a short shelf life.
- Food is stored between 0 and 8°C. Ideal is 4°C.

Cook-chill

- Food is prepared, cooked, portioned. Rapid chilling starts within 30 minutes of cooking, to between 0 and 3°C in 90 minutes or less.
- Sold from chilled cabinets (8°C is maximum legal temperature; 5°C is ideal temperature)
- Shelf life is five days if kept in a refrigerator.
- If reheated, food must be heated to at least 72°C.

Advantages of cook-chill:

- It is considered to be of a higher quality than frozen food.
- No defrosting is required.
- There is very little change in nutritive value, flavour, texture or shape.
- A wide range of foods is available.
- Fewer additives are required during manufacture.
- Food is available in single portions.
- No skill is required – easy to prepare and cook.
- Minimal equipment and washing up needed.
- The quality is consistent.
- There is little waste.
- Saves on energy in the home.

> **examiner tip**
> Remember the time and temperature for chilling.

Freezing

- Food is stored in freezer, between −18 and −29°C.
- No water is available for micro-organisms to grow.
- Food is quick frozen to produce small ice crystals – so there is less damage to cell structure.
- There is little change in nutritive value.
- A large range of foods is available.
- Frozen foods have a longer shelf life than chilled products.

Blast freezing is suitable for most foods. Air is circulated by a fan, reducing the temperature of the food quickly. With the cook-freeze method, meals are blast frozen and stored at −20°C until required.
Chilled and frozen foods are transported in refrigerated vans.

Dehydration (drying)

Water is removed so micro-organisms cannot grow. Colour, flavour, texture and nutritive value may be affected. Food can be dried by:

- direct sunlight, e.g. raisins
- heating gently in an oven, e.g. herbs
- spray drying, e.g. milk
- roller drying, e.g. breakfast cereals.

Accelerated Freeze Drying (AFD) is combination of freezing and drying. Food is quickly frozen, then placed in a vacuum under reduced pressure. Little change in colour, flavour, texture and nutritive value. Light to carry, easy to rehydrate.

Other methods of preserving

Revised

Other methods include:

- chemicals – to prevent bacteria from growing
- vinegar – bacteria cannot survive the acid level
- salt – as a coating, e.g. ham or brine solution (salt and water), reduces moisture content
- sugar – in high concentrations, e.g. jam
- **additives** – destroy bacteria or prevent them reproducing.

Modified atmosphere packaging (MAP)

Figure 21.2 Sugar is used in high concentrations to preserve food such as jam

Figure 21.3 Using MAP to package apples

- Air is removed.
- Food is resealed in a mixture of oxygen, nitrogen and carbon dioxide.
- Once opened, food has a normal shelf life, e.g. chilled meats, fruits.

Vacuum-packed food

- Air is removed.
- Packaging is sealed, which prevents bacteria growing.
- Once opened, food has a normal shelf life.
- The **anaerobic** conditions (no oxygen) means that food maintains its colour, flavour, texture, e.g. bacon.

Check your understanding
Tested

1 State the correct temperature for a refrigerator. (1 mark)
2 Give **two** reasons why the temperature of chill cabinets is regularly checked in shops. (2 marks)
3 Give **three** benefits to the consumer of cook-chill products. (3 marks)
4 Describe how freezing increases the shelf life of vegetables. (2 marks)
5 Give **two** reasons why manufacturers need to consider the shelf life of a product. (2 marks)

22 Packaging of food products

Reasons why food is packaged

- Packaging contains the product so that it is easy to transport, store and display.
- When sealed, it prevents spillage and loss.
- It identifies the product. Labelling information is required by law.
- Packaging helps to promote the product and attract customers
- It protects the product from damage, e.g. being crushed, from chemicals, insects, from atmospheric conditions, so reduces waste.
- It increases the shelf life of the product.

Packaging materials

Packaging material	Benefits/advantages	Limitations/disadvantages	Examples of food
Glass	Moulded in a variety of shapes Transparent – can see product Withstands high temperatures Strong Recyclable Cheap to produce	Brittle and will often break easily Heavy	Jam, sauces, pickles
Metals including foil and cans	Strong Withstands high temperatures Lightweight Different thicknesses Recyclable Moulded into a variety of shapes Easy to store	Cannot see the food Cannot be used in the microwave Not sustainable	Canned foods, e.g. fruit, soup, meat, fish, ready meals
Plastic	Cheap to produce Moulded into a variety of shapes Different thicknesses Can be used in the microwave Easy to print on Lightweight Some are biodegradable Most do not react with foods Transparent – can see product Withstands high temperatures	Can be difficult to dispose of Made initially from oil A lot is still not recyclable – non-renewable source	Yogurts, cheese, bread, fruit, vegetables, ready meals, biscuits
Paper/card	Cheap to produce Different thicknesses Easy to open Recyclable Easy to print on Lightweight Variety of shapes Biodegradable Can be made from recycled material	Can tear easily Not waterproof unless it is laminated Product could be easily crushed and damaged	Cereals, eggs, flour, sugar, baked products, e.g. cakes, biscuits, pizza
Ovenable paperboard	Used in the oven and microwave Easy to print on Lightweight	Loses shape and strength when soggy Easily crushed so damaging the product	Frozen and chilled meals

Table 22.1 Advantages and disadvantages of packaging materials

Aseptic cartons and 'tamper-evident' packaging

With **aseptic** cartons and '**tamper-evident**' packaging:

- Plastic can be combined with other materials.
- Plastic can be laminated – this means coating with layers of other materials, such as card or aluminium. Using laminated materials in packaging can reduce the need for food preservatives and extend the shelf life of the product.
- Combining different materials makes the packaging currently not suitable for recycling.
- Examples include long-life orange juice and milk.

Figure 22.1 Cartons

Figure 22.2 Tamper-evident packaging

Tamper-evident techniques make it easier to see if the packaging has been opened, so reducing the risk of the food becoming contaminated e.g. plastic collars on sauce bottles; film overwraps on cardboard boxes; tear-away strips around the top of plastic bottles. If seals are broken, do not buy the product.

Manufacturers, retailers and consumers all need to be aware of the environmental issues involved in producing, using and disposing of such a large amount of packaging. (See also Chapter 35.)

> **examiner tip**
>
> Before your exam, find out about new packaging materials being used in the food industry.

Check your understanding

Tested

1 State **one** different advantage for *each* of the following packaging materials:
   a) plastic
   b) metal
   c) paperboard. (3 marks)
2 Give **two** reasons why food is packaged. (2 marks)
3 State **one** different method of packaging for each of the following products:
   a) eggs
   b) oranges
   c) fruit juice. (3 marks)
4 State **two** ways packaging can be made attractive to the consumer. (2 marks)
5 State **one** reason why manufacturers might use **tamper-evident** packaging. (1 mark)

23 Labelling of food products

Information required on a label by law

Revised

Information	Reason
Product name and description	This describes what the product is.
List of ingredients	Listed in descending order of weight, largest amount first. Information about food additives and water must be included.
Storage instructions	Explains how to store to prevent food spoilage.
Date marking	Length of time the product can be kept.
Manufacturer's name and address	Provided in case customer wants to return product or write letter of complaint.
Weight or volume	Used for most pre-packed food. If not pre-packed, it is sold by quantity or number. Some products are sold in standard amounts so that consumers can compare products, i.e. value for money. A large **e** shows an average quantity. **e 190g**
Instructions for use	Preparation, cooking and heating instructions.
Place of origin	The place where the food has come from.
Allergies	Any ingredients that may cause reactions in people with allergies.

Table 23.1 Information required on a label

Date marking

Revised

- 'Use by' date – used for high-risk foods. It includes day and month. After this, may not look or taste different but unsafe to eat.

- 'Best Before Date' – used for low-risk foods. It includes the day, month and year. After this, flavour, colour, texture deteriorates.

- 'Display until' date – this is a few days before the 'use by' date. It informs the retailer when to remove product from shelves or chill/freezer cabinets for stock control.

> **examiner tip**
> Revise this list before your exam.

Date marking (i.e. 'use by' and 'best before') is determined by:

- microbiologists, who examine bacterial growth and identify a safe shelf life.
- food technologists, who assess food by taste testing and by how long the product maintains its qualities.

Other information found on packaging

Revised

Information	Reason
Barcode	Identifies product. Helps retailer with stock control. Electronic scanner at checkout reads bar code; records and displays price.
Nutritional Information	Allows consumers to: See nutritional content – informed choices can be made. Select according to specific nutrient content, e.g. low in sugar. Compare nutritional content of products. Not required unless a special claim is made, e.g. 'low in fat'.
Serving Instructions	Serving ideas
Cost	Can compare price of different products.

Table 23.2 Other information found on packaging

Some manufacturers use a traffic light colour system, which enables customers to see quickly if the product is low, medium or high in fat, sugar and salt.

Other information placed on packaging voluntarily by some manufacturers includes logos that inform consumers about recycling and sustainability.

How packaging and labelling help prevent food poisoning   Revised

Labelling:

- Listing ingredients identifies high-risk foods.
- Gives correct storage conditions – where the food should be stored and for how long.
- Best before/use by dates state for how long the food will be safe to eat.
- Cooking instructions explain the method and temperature required for cooking.

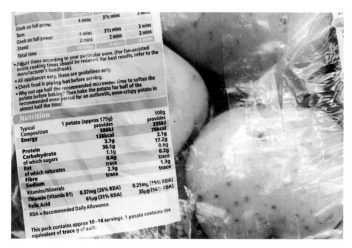

Figure 23.1 Nutritional labelling

Packaging:

- Packaging protects from damage/contamination.
- The choice of material should suit cooking method/ storage.
- **Impermeable** materials are used for some foods. Some foods need to be airtight.
- Some foods need to be packaged using **modified atmosphere packaging (MAP)**.
- Some materials can extend shelf life, for example, for foods that are heat processed (e.g. pasteurised milk in glass).
- When sealed, plastics can prevent contamination.

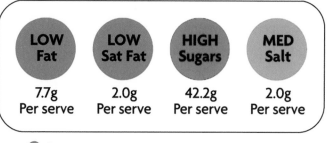

Green = Low
Amber = Medium
Red = High

Figure 23.2 Traffic light system (Source: Food Standards Agency)

Check your understanding   Tested

1 State **three** pieces of information that must by law be on packaging. (3 marks)
2 Give **one** reason why a bar code is used on food packaging. (1 mark)
3 Give **two** benefits to the consumer of having nutritional information on packaging. (2 marks)
4 Explain **two** ways how packaging can help prevent food poisoning. (4 marks)
5 Explain **two** ways how labelling of food products can help prevent food poisoning. (4 marks)

24 Hygiene practices

Safe hygiene practices

Revised ☐

Practice	How to ensure safety
Buying food	Buy from a reputable shop Food should look fresh, and be within date mark
Transporting food	Food should be packaged so not damaged during transit Perishable food should be kept chilled, below 8°C and transported quickly, using insulated lorries Frozen food should be transported by specialist freezer lorries Chilled and frozen food should be transported home in cool bags
Storage of food	Frozen food should be kept in freezer; chilled and perishable food in fridge; non-perishable food (e.g. canned) in cool, dry, well-ventilated cupboard
Preparing food	Leave **perishables** in fridge until ready for use Defrost frozen foods before preparation Clean work surfaces before and after preparation Wash fruits and vegetables before using Avoid **cross-contamination**, e.g. use colour-coded chopping boards
Cooking food	Cook thoroughly If keeping food hot, it must be at or above 63°C. Use a temperature (food) probe to test internal temperature

Table 24.1 Ways of ensuring safe hygiene

Food poisoning

Revised ☐

Poor hygiene practices can lead to contamination and possibly food poisoning.
Bacteria causing food poisoning are called **pathenogenic bacteria**.

Contamination occurs because of:

- poor personal hygiene practice by food handlers
- poor hygiene during production and serving
- cross-contamination between raw and cooked foods
- storing high-risk foods at room temperature
- poor preparation and cooking routines, such as:
  - inadequate thawing
  - preparing food too far in advance
  - under cooking high risk foods
  - insufficient cooling before placing in chill cabinets or freezers
  - not reheating foods to the correct temperature for long enough
  - keeping 'hot' foods below 63°C
  - leaving food on display at room temperature for longer than four hours.

> **examiner tip**
>
> Check whether the question is asking about transporting, storage, preparing or cooking.

Other reasons for an increase in food poisoning include:

- increased use of microwaves – food not always defrosted or cooked/reheated correctly
- more people eating out
- increased use of cook-chill and frozen products

Some people, e.g. pregnant women and older people, are more susceptible to food poisoning. Take extra care when preparing and cooking food for these groups.

The symptoms of food poisoning are diarrhoea, vomiting, nausea, headache and fever.

Food poisoning bacteria	Possible sources
Salmonella	Poultry, eggs, meat
Staphylococcus	Food handlers
Clostridium	Raw foods, e.g. vegetables, meat
Bacillus	Cereals, especially rice
Campylobacter	Infected animals, birds and unpasteurised milk
Listeria	Raw, processed and cooked foods, e.g. soft cheese
E.Coli	Cattle, raw meat and raw milk

Table 24.2 Possible sources of food poisoning bacteria

Cross-contamination — Revised

Micro-organisms can transfer from raw to cooked foods, causing infection. This is known as cross-contamination. Food should be prepared in separate areas using different-coloured chopping boards and knives.

To prevent cross-contamination, avoid:

- raw and cooked foods touching each other
- blood and juices of raw foods dripping onto cooked foods
- bacteria being transferred during handling.

Rules for food hygiene — Revised

1 Wash hands thoroughly before handling and between handling different types of food.
2 Keep raw and cooked foods separate and use different equipment to prepare them.
3 Wear clean protective clothing, cover cuts and never cough or sneeze over food.
4 Keep working surfaces and utensils clean. Wash surfaces and utensils between tasks.
5 Cover and cool cooked food rapidly and refrigerate quickly.
6 Do not put hot foods in the refrigerator.
7 Keep pets away from food preparation areas.
8 Keep bins covered and empty and wash them regularly.
9 Reheat food thoroughly above 72°C. Take care to avoid 'cold spots' when heating in a microwave – turn and move the food.

Figure 24.2 Would these bins be acceptable in your kitchen?

Check your understanding — Tested

1 State what is meant by cross-contamination. (1 mark)
2 State the type of bacteria that causes food poisoning. (1 mark)
3 Give **three** rules to prevent cross-contamination. (3 marks)
4 Explain **two** issues that must be considered when transporting food products. (4 marks)
5 Explain why there has been an increase in the number of reported cases of food poisoning. (4 marks)

25 Risk assessment and environmental health

What is risk assessment?
Revised

- Risk assessment is a careful examination of what could cause harm. In the food industry, one of the areas where a risk assessment must be done is food production. This means that activities that take place during food production must be assessed for the risk of harm and the required action taken to ensure that food is safe to eat.
- The risk assessment system used within the food industry is known as the Hazard Analysis Critical Control Point (**HACCP**).
- HACCP identifies specific hazards and risks associated with food production and describes how these hazards and risks can be controlled.

Hazards can emerge at any stage of food production and distribution:

Raw foods/materials $\longrightarrow$ Making $\longrightarrow$ Distribution $\longrightarrow$ Supermarket

A hazard is anything that can cause harm to a consumer. A hazard may be:

- biological, e.g. salmonella in chicken
- chemical, e.g. cleaning chemicals getting into food
- physical, e.g. glass or metal getting into food.

A risk is the likelihood that a hazard might occur.

Critical control point (CCP)

A critical control point is a step in the making process where a control must be in place to manage hazards. Some hazards, e.g. micro-biological, are high-risk. It is critical (essential) that the hazard is removed or reduced because it could result in food poisoning.

> **examiner tip**
> Link this to computer-controlled sensors. Where are checks made?

Benefits of HACCP to the food industry
Revised

- HACCP predicts hazards.
- It is preventive rather than responding to problems as they occur.
- It saves money by planning ahead.
- Critical control points mean that people are focusing on the important problems.
- Response can be rapid.
- It supports '**due diligence**', i.e. proving that all reasonable precautions have been taken.
- All staff are involved with product safety.
- It helps make safe food products.
- It helps the industry to meet legal requirements for safety.

Examples of areas of risk
Revised

- Temperature control – from storage of raw materials through to preparation and service of food.
- During cleaning and disinfection of preparation areas, etc.
- Hygiene – personal hygiene, staff training.

- Control systems – stock rotation, pest control, quality control, waste disposal, how cross-contamination is avoided.
- Poorly designed premises – lighting, ventilation, washing facilities, etc.

The role of Environmental Health Officers (EHO) — Revised

On every visit the EHO will carry out a risk assessment. Most companies are visited every nine months to a year.

The role of Environmental Health Officers is to:
- enforce food safety laws
- ensure that food is safe and fit to eat
- aim to reduce possible sources of contamination
- monitor working conditions and hygiene systems
- offer advice and support.

Environmental Health Officers have the power to:
- visit and inspect food premises at any reasonable time, without notice, to ensure businesses are operating safely and hygienically
- visit as a result of a complaint
- look at records, take photographs and/or remove samples
- issue notices to improve conditions or stop certain practices
- close part or all of a business if necessary
- seize and detain food
- prosecute employers and employees.

Check your understanding — Tested

1 Explain what is meant by risk assessment. (2 marks)
2 State what is meant by HACCP. (1 mark)
3 Explain what is meant by 'due diligence'. (1 mark)
4 Describe the role of the Environmental Health Officer. (4 marks)
5 Explain what is meant by a critical control point. (2 marks)

Food safety

26 Food safety

Food safety law

Revised

Several laws cover the regulations for the preparation, storage and sale of food.
The main offences include selling or keeping for sale food that:

- is unfit for human consumption.
- has been made harmful to health.
- is contaminated.
- is not of the nature, substance or quality expected.
- is falsely or misleadingly presented.

The law on food safety is enforced by Environmental Health Officers and the Trading Standards Office.

All premises have to be registered. All staff must have training in food hygiene.

When these Acts are adhered to, food businesses have satisfied customers, a good reputation and consequently increased business. There is less wastage of food, because food has an increased shelf life, resulting in higher profits.

Key points

- Food preparation areas should be clean and in good repair.
- Surfaces must be smooth, easy to clean and disinfect.
- There should be adequate cleaning and **disinfection**.
- There should be adequate lighting and ventilation.
- Floors and walls must be non-absorbent and stay clean.
- Open windows should be designed to prevent insects entering
- Pest control policy must be in place.
- Quality control checks must be done on ingredients.
- Food must be stored in hygienic conditions and protected from **contamination**.
- Adequate toilets and wash hand basins must be provided.
- Drinking water must be available.
- Core temperatures must be recorded during cooking.
- Equipment must be colour coded.
- Equipment and packaging must be clean and made of a material that is easily disinfected.
- Food waste must be removed regularly.
- Bins must be: kept in good condition, easy to clean and disinfect, fitted with lids and kept away from food stores and equipment.

Figure 26.1 Handle food hygienically

Food handlers must:

- be trained in food hygiene
- maintain a good standard of personal hygiene
- wear clean, protective clothing as appropriate, e.g. a hat, gloves, boots, beard shield
- report illness to their supervisor
- rewash hands when moving from low-risk to high-risk areas.

examiner tip

Read the question carefully to check whether it is asking about equipment or about food workers.

Food handlers must not:

- work if suffering from illness
- wear jewellery.

Temperature control and transportation

Revised

Temperature control

Regulations clarify three systems of temperature control:

a) Chill holding. Food to be kept at 8°C or below. Good practice is 5°C.

b) Hot holding. Reheated food should not be kept. If kept hot – temperature of 63°C or above.

c) Reheating of food. Must be reheated to 72°C or higher.

Transportation

- Vehicles must be clean, in good condition.
- Temperature-controlled vehicles are designed so that the temperature can easily be monitored and controlled. Food should be stored to prevent growth of micro-organisms: below 8°C in a refrigerated van and below −18°C in a freezer van.
- A distribution system should be established to record orders and delivery dates.

examiner tip

For high marks, always give the temperatures.

Figure 26.2 Refrigerated lorries

Date marking

Revised

Virtually all packaged foods carry a date mark, either in the form of 'use by' or 'best before' dates (see Chapter 23).

Check your understanding

Tested

1 State who monitors and enforces the law in food production. (1 mark)
2 Give **three** personal hygiene rules that workers should follow. (3 marks)
3 Explain why colour-coded equipment should be used in the kitchen. (2 marks)
4 State the temperature required when reheating food. (1 mark)
5 Explain how legislation can ensure health and safety in the food industry. (5 marks)

27 CAD, CAM, quality assurance and quality control

Computer-aided design (CAD)

Computers are used for:

- desk research – looking at statistics, e.g. eating trends
- carrying out and analysing data from sensory evaluation
- modelling costs/nutritional analysis/ratio and proportions of ingredients
- designing packaging and labels, advertising.

Advantages/benefits of CAD

- Greater accuracy, e.g. working out nutritional analysis.
- Professional finish, e.g. graphics/art work on packaging.
- Tasks can be completed quickly, e.g. annotated drawings; graphical work for packaging.
- Colours and graphic effects can be modelled and tried out. Designs can easily be varied when product changes.
- Modelling of recipes without wasting money trialling products.
- Designs sent quickly by email from design to manufacturing stage.

Figure 27.1 Computers play an important role

> **examiner tip**
> Many candidates muddle CAD and CAM. Make sure you know the difference.

Computer-aided making (CAM)

In computer-aided making, production systems are controlled by computer.

Advantages/benefits of using CAM	Examples
Saves time	Repetitive tasks carried out quickly, e.g. cutting pastry tops
Standardises production	Gives accuracy and precision so that a consistent finish is maintained, e.g. thickness of biscuits
Increases productivity	Products made at speed, lowering costs
Increases reliability of finished products	All stages of production are controlled.
Monitors production system	Sensors detect and record critical control points, e.g. weight, temperature
Reduces storage	'Just in time' system used, so nothing made in advance and the need for storage is minimised
Increases safety	Workers do not carry out hazardous tasks
High standard of packaging	Cutting nets. Printing labelling information
Deals with large amount of information	Monitoring complex production schedules, e.g. HACCP, stock control

Table 27.1 The advantages of CAM

Effects of CAD/CAM on workforce

- Staff need training to operate computerised equipment.
- Numbers of staff may be reduced.
- Staff costs may be higher as they do more responsible and skilled jobs.
- Engineers are required.
- There may be problems if the computer system breaks down.
- Jobs could become monotonous and boring.

Figure 27.2 Preparing dough for bread using computer-controlled equipment

Quality

Revised

Quality assurance

Quality assurance gives a 'a level of guarantee' or 'positive declaration'. Manufacturers set criteria and specifications for every stage of designing and production. Checks include: specification checks, hygiene procedures, monitoring waste and sensory analysis.

Quality control

Quality control is part of the quality assurance system. Involves checking standards, including critical control points (HACCP), during design and manufacture so that product specifications are met.

Computer-controlled sensors

Revised

All of the following can be carried out by computer-controlled sensors:

- sorting and grading raw materials
- stock control of raw ingredients and components
- weighing ingredients
- correct consistency of a dough
- thickness of a dough
- flow rates, e.g. chocolate coatings
- cutting dough into accurate portions/size/shape.
- temperature control during storage, baking and chilling/use of food probe
- time control during cooking
- colour sensor, e.g. degree of brownness of finished bread products
- decorations and shapes – visual images stored on the computer, e.g. positioning of toppings on cakes
- counting into packages
- sealing packages
- metal detector, e.g. nuts or screws falling into a mixture
- weighing finished product
- moisture sensor – correct texture/moisture content, e.g. during storage
- pH level – important to the shelf life
- bacterial content.

> **examiner tip**
>
> Computer-controlled sensors can be used for quality control and also for food safety.

Check your understanding

Tested

1 State **two** ways that CAD can be used in the food industry. (2 marks)
2 Give **two** advantages of using CAD. (2 marks)
3 State what is meant by quality assurance. (1 mark)
4 A food manufacturer wants to produce a batch of 50 fruit pies. State **three** quality control checks that the manufacture could carry out to make sure that all the pies are identical. (3 marks)
5 State **one** reason for using CAM in each of the following processes in the production of chocolate biscuits:
   a) weighing
   b) baking
   c) coating (3 marks)

28 Commercial production methods

Several different production methods are used in the food industry. The method used depends on the food product being produced.

Job/craft/one-off

The job/craft/one-off method is when one product is made. Examples include wedding and other celebration cakes.

Benefits/advantages of job/craft/one-off:

- The products are individual or even unique.
- The products are of a high quality.

Limitations/disadvantages:

- Skilled staff are required.
- It is time consuming – processes are done by hand.
- It can be expensive.

Batch

The batch method is used for small numbers of identical or similar products.

Figure 28.1 Wedding cake made using job/craft/one-off production

Examples include teacakes and Chelsea buns.

Benefits/advantages of the batch method:

- Small orders can be made.
- Equipment can be used for a variety of products.
- Slight adaptations can be made without too much cost to meet consumer demand, e.g. different fillings for pies.
- Raw materials are bought in bulk.
- Production costs are lower than with the job/craft/one-off method.
- Only a small number of people are involved.

Limitation/disadvantage:

- Waste can be high if the process fails.

Mass

The mass method is used to make large numbers of one product. The process is split into tasks and sequenced into an assembly line using conveyor belts. Specialised equipment or line operators carry out tasks.

Figure 28.2 Preparing bread using batch production

Examples include sliced loaves, digestive biscuits, crisps, sandwiches.

Benefits/advantages of the mass method:

- Orders are quickly and efficiently met.
- Raw materials are bought in bulk, which reduces costs.
- The ratio of workers to production is low.
- Workers do not have to be highly skilled.
- Parts or all the line can be automated.

examiner tip

Make sure you read the question. Is it asking for a benefit or a limitation?

- Large numbers of products can be made at low cost.
- The production line can be altered to make another product.

Limitations/disadvantages:

- Maintenance checks must be thorough and regular to avoid breakdowns, which would be expensive due to in lost production.
- The initial set up is expensive as large-scale specialist equipment is required.
- Tasks can be repetitive and boring for workers.

Continuous-flow — Revised

The **continuous-flow** method is computer controlled to produce one specific product in large quantities, non-stop, 24 hours a day. Examples include soft drinks and milk.

Figure 28.3 A mass-produced product

Benefits/advantages:

- It is cheap to run.
- High quality products are produced.
- A small workforce is needed.
- Product quality is consistent.
- Orders are quickly and efficiently met.
- Raw materials are bought in bulk, which reduces costs.

Limitations/disadvantages:

- Maintenance checks must be thorough and regular to avoid breakdowns, which would be expensive due to lost production.
- The initial set up is expensive as large-scale specialist equipment is required.
- Tasks can be repetitive and boring for workers.

Figure 28.4 Production on a continuous flow production line

Check your understanding — Tested

1 State **two** advantages to a manufacturer of batch production. (2 marks)
2 Oven chips are a food product that can be manufactured using continuous flow. State **one** advantage of continuous flow. (1 mark)
3 State **one** limitation/disadvantage of continuous flow. (1 mark)
4 State **two** advantages to the consumer of buying a one-off/craft food product. (2 marks)
5 State **two** disadvantages to the consumer of buying a one-off/craft food product. (2 marks)

29 Design process

New products are developed according to consumers' changing needs and new trends. This is done by adapting an existing product or by developing a completely new and original product.

Market research
Revised

There are two kinds of research material:

- **primary** – interviews, questionnaires, sensory testing, evaluating existing food products.
- **secondary** – books, newspapers, recipe books, magazines, websites, leaflets.

Questionnaires and interviews are designed to extract specific information about the qualities required in a new product.

Questionnaires should start with an introduction, to encourage respondents to:

- focus on the purpose of the questionnaire
- feel involved from the start so that they give satisfactory responses.

The results should be easy to collate and analyse into a report. A written report can include graphs (e.g. pie chart/bar graph) tally charts, table of results. These can be presented in PowerPoint.

A **design specification** can then be developed. A design specification clearly states the general criteria for the product to be developed.

Generating and communicating ideas
Revised

- Use recipe books.
- Look at existing products.
- Use websites.

Communicate ideas by means of:

- word-processed documents
- annotated sketches
- mood boards
- analysis of nutritional printouts
- sensory analysis charts
- photographs of practical products.

Figure 29.1 Recipe books

> ### examiner tip
> Think about the work you completed for your Controlled Assessments.

Figure 29.2 Photo of a practical product

Recipes may be adapted to alter nutritional content, shape, flavour, texture etc.

Sensory analysis testing is carried out throughout the whole design and making process to monitor qualities and identify improvements. (See also Chapter 30.)

Initial trialled ideas are evaluated against a design specification, using evidence from sensory analysis to:

- identify how each idea has met the criteria
- select a suitable idea for product development
- identify any improvements.

Product development is all about changing, testing or modifying all or part of a product, taking into account users' views, until a desired outcome is achieved and a product specification can be developed. A product specification describes the very specific characteristics a product must have.

examiner tip

You may be required to adapt a given recipe and/or suggest improvements from results of sensory testing. Answers often require you to give reasons for your suggestions.

examiner tip

If you are asked for more than one way of advertising and promoting products, make sure you include more than one way in your answer.

Advertising and promotions   Revised

There are many different ways of advertising and promoting food products, including:

- advertisements on TV, in cinemas, newspapers, internet, posters etc.
- displays in supermarkets
- special offers, e.g. 'buy one get one free' ('bogof'), money-off coupons
- celebrity endorsements by sports or pop stars
- competitions
- free samples
- free gifts
- eye-catching, attractive packaging.

Check your understanding   Tested

1 State **two** methods of identifying a gap in the market before developing a new food product. (2 marks)
2 State **one** research method a manufacturer may use when generating new ideas. (1 mark)
3 Explain why sensory analysis testing is important when generating and modelling ideas. (2 marks)
4 Explain the difference between a design specification and a product specification. (2 marks)
5 A supermarket has identified a gap in the market for a new pasta product. The design specification for the new pasta product is as follows: the product must be colourful and high in fibre; have a variety of textures; and include protein. Draw **one** idea that could meet the design specification. State how your design meets each specification point. (4 marks)

30 Sensory analysis

Why sensory analysis testing is carried out on food products

- Sensory analysis testing allows manufacturers to monitor **organoleptic** qualities.
- It enables modifications (changes) to be made throughout development so that the final product is successful.
- The product can be matched against the specification.
- It finds out consumers' likes/wants.
- It tests shelf life/keeping qualities.
- It helps maintain a consistently high-standard product.
- Products can be compared with those of competitors.

Sensory analysis tests

Ranking tests are used to rank samples in order, for example:

- a specific attribute (e.g. sweetness)
- preference of taste
- sometimes a descriptor is used, e.g. ranking crisps in order of saltiness.

Taste the samples and put them in the order you like best		
Sample code	Order	Comments
1		
2		
3		
4		

Table 30.1 An example of a ranking test

Rating tests can be used to show how much tasters like or dislike several aspects of one product as shown in the table below.

Criteria	Votes by tasting panel (1 = poor, 2 = average, 3 = good, 4 = v good, 5 = excellent)					Total	Average
Flavour	4	4	5	3	4	20	4
Thickness	1	1	2	1	2	7	1.4
Colour	3	4	1	5	2	15	3
Smoothness	3	2	1	2	3	11	2.2

Table 30.2 Rating using a descriptor

Another way of showing the results of a rating test is a star profile. This describes the appearance, taste and texture of a food product.

During sensory profiling testing in industry:

- Six or more trained assessors are used.
- Each assessor rates the intensity of each descriptor on a scale (one is the lowest).
- Results from each assessor are added up and the average rating for each descriptor is worked out.
- A visual profile is created by plotting the results on a spider or star diagram.

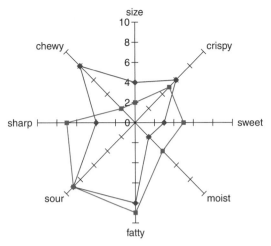

Figure 30.1 Profile of a citrus cookie

In a triangle test, three samples are given with two being identical and the third slightly different. The testers are asked to identify the 'odd one out'.

Carrying out sensory analysis testing — Revised

- Set up a quiet area where people will not be disturbed – communication is not allowed.
- Give a drink of lemon-flavoured water or a piece of apple to clear the palate.
- Use small quantities of food on plain, identical sized plates/dishes.
- Use coloured lighting.
- Use same garnish or decoration.
- Try not to give too many samples at once.
- Serve at correct temperature for the product being tested.
- Use clean spoons or forks each time.
- Use codes for products to prevent testers being influenced by the name of the product (known as testing blind).
- Have charts ready before testing begins.
- Make sure testers know how to complete the charts.

Check your understanding — Tested

1 State **two** ways a food manufacturer could use results from sensory analysis testing when developing a product. (2 marks)

2 Explain the difference between a rating and a ranking test. (2 marks)

3 Explain what is meant by a triangle test. (2 marks)

4 The table below shows the results of a product tasting panel for a cheese and herb muffin

Criteria	Votes by tasting panel (1 = poor, 2 = average, 3 = good, 4 = v good, 5 = excellent)					Total
Soft texture	4	4	5	5	5	23
Herb flavour	1	2	2	1	2	8
Golden brown	5	5	5	5	4	24
Well risen	5	5	4	4	4	22
Cheese flavour	3	3	2	1	2	11

Table 30.3 Results of a product tasting panel for a cheese and herb muffin

a) State the **two** areas that need to be improved.

b) Suggest how **one** of these areas could be improved.

c) Suggest **one** other way the results from the tasting panel could be presented. (4 marks)

31 Product analysis

The reasons for carrying out product analysis are to:

- analyse all aspects of a product in detail
- decide how suitable a product is for an intended market
- gain ideas for new products
- compare differences in brands
- decide what ingredients and components are in a product
- investigate how the product is made
- understand the processes used to make the product
- check that a product meets its specification
- consider the moral, cultural, environmental and sustainability issues involved in the production.

Guidelines for carrying out product analysis   Revised

- Who is the product aimed at and why?
- What is the purpose of the product? When, where, why and how will it be eaten?
- What ingredients, components, additives have been used in the product and why?
- What processes have been used in making it?
- How has it been made safe to eat?
- How does it fit the Eatwell Plate?
- How well does it meet the nutritional and identified needs of the target group?
- Does it have any special claims, such as low in fat?
- How has it been made to appeal to the target group?
- What is the cost of the product? Is it in the correct price range for the user?
- How does the product compare with similar ones available?
- Has the manufacturer considered the environmental, moral, cultural and sustainability issues within the product?

Analysing a product   Revised

The following is a list of points that you might consider when carrying out a product analysis of a chicken and ham pie.

Figure 31.1 Chicken and ham pie

Who would buy this product? Why?	Families, because it is a ready-cooked, quick meal.
Who could not eat the pie?	People with coeliac disease (it contains flour). People on a fat-reduced diet as it is high in fat
What type of pastry is used?	Puff pastry
What ingredients have been used in the pastry?	Flour/fat
What other ingredients have been added to the chicken filling? Why?	Ham to give flavour, gravy for moistness
Has the pie got a base? What is the proportion of pastry to filling?	The pastry base makes the ratio of pastry to meat high and so the pie is much cheaper to produce than one with more meat in it.
Why might the quantity of pastry be reduced?	It would have less saturated fat in if it only had a top, not a base.
How could the design be improved to meet healthy eating guidelines?	Reduce the quantity of pastry by using only a top. Add vegetables (e.g. peas, peppers). Use mushrooms instead of ham.

examiner tip

Make sure that you name ingredients properly. Don't just put 'vegetables': you must name them.

Check your understanding

Tested

1 Figure 31.2 shows a packet of cheese sandwiches bought from a supermarket.
   a) State **two** groups of people who would buy these sandwiches (2 marks)
   b) Give **two** ways of increasing the fibre in the sandwiches. (2 marks)
   c) State **two** reasons why the sandwiches are packaged. (2 marks)
2 Figure 31.3 shows a picture of a milk-based fruit dessert.

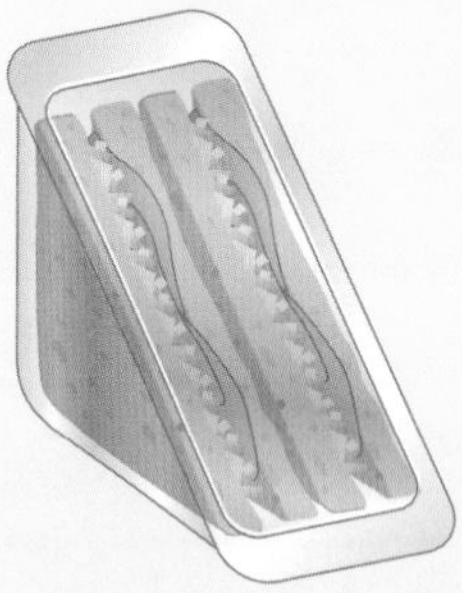

Figure 31.2 Grated Cheddar cheese and cooked ham in white bread spread with English butter

Figure 31.3 Milk-based fruit dessert

   a) State **one** target group for the milk dessert. (1 mark)
   b) Give **two** reasons why this dessert is suitable for that target group (2 marks)
   c) State how the dessert should be stored at home. (1 mark)
3 State **two** commercial processing methods that will extend the shelf life of milk products. (2 marks)
4 A manufacturer wants to increase sales of desserts. State **two** ways that desserts could be promoted to appeal to children. (2 marks)

32 The six Rs

Recycle

Recycling means reprocessing a material or product to make something else.

Types of recycling

Primary recycling

- Using a plastic carrier bag as a bin liner
- Using ice cream tubs or margarine cartons to store dry ingredients
- Glass jars reused for storage or homemade jams and pickles
- Re-using carrier bags for shopping
- Eating leftover food – this can be classed as recycling as well as re-using.

Secondary or physical recycling

- Raw vegetable waste can be composted

Tertiary or chemical recycling

- Plastic bottles can be recycled into fibres
- **Composting**

Recyclable materials used include:

- glass
- paper
- metals
- some plastics
- food waste.

Figure 32.1 Re-use of a carrier bag

Figure 32.2 Adding a teabag to a composting bin

Reuse

- Products that can be reused for either the same purpose or as a new product.
- When food waste cannot be reused it ends up in landfill sites, it rots and produces **methane**.
- Raw waste can be composted but it is not so easy to reuse leftover foods.
- Use left-over food to make another dish instead of throwing it away.
- In the UK we throw away over 6.7 million tons of food each year.
- Food cannot be reused in industry because of food hygiene regulations.

Reduce

Reduce the effects of poor diet on health:

- Use and adapt recipes so that meals are low in fat, salt and sugar.
- Follow the advice given in the **Eatwell Plate**.

Reduce the use of processed foods:

- Processed foods require a lot of energy to produce them.
- They are often high in fats, salt and sugar.
- They have at least two layers of packaging, using more resources.
- Each stage of the process has an impact upon the environment; this will contribute to the product's **carbon footprint**.

Figure 32.3 Trifle

Reduce the energy used in cooking:

- The cost of energy is rising.
- Most of the energy used in the UK comes from **unsustainable** sources.

Reduce food waste:

- Plan what you are going to eat for each meal.
- Shop using a shopping list.
- Freeze excess food.
- Use left-over food.

Reduce the use of pesticides. (See Chapter 35.)

Refuse
Revised

Packaging

- Refuse over-packaged foods – discarded packaging creates waste and often ends up in **landfill sites**.
- Even if packaging is recyclable, the recycling process uses energy.

Diet

- Refuse food that is high in fat, salt and sugar. (See Chapter 12.)
- If we eat a balanced diet we are less likely to get heart disease, diabetes, osteoporosis, diverticulosis and some cancers.

Rethink
Revised

Rethink the average UK high-fat diet:

- The number of people with diet-related illnesses continues to rise – we should reduce the amount of fat we eat.

Rethink the use of healthy ingredients in creative designs:

- There is a wide range of fruits and vegetables available to use in recipes, as well as many different pulses, nuts and cereal grains.
- Many of these ingredients will not only improve the nutritional content but also the taste, texture, colour and aroma of a product.

Rethink where we source our ingredients:

- Use seasonal produce – grown in the UK.
- Buy local produce.
- Consider growing your own food.

Figure 32.4 High street shopping

> **examiner tip**
>
> When answering questions make sure you give specific examples. Avoid using phrases such as 'It's more environmentally friendly.'

Repair
Revised

Nutrients help repair and maintain a healthy body. (See Chapter 1.)

Check your understanding
Tested

1. State the **three** different types of recycling. (3 marks)
2. Give **two** reasons why we should consider reducing the amount of energy used when cooking food. (2 marks)
3. Explain why we should reduce the amount of fat, salt and sugar we consume. (6 marks)
4. Explain why we should refuse to purchase over-packaged products. (4 marks)
5. State **four** rules which you should follow when reusing foods. (4 marks)

Moral issues

33 Moral issues

In food technology, the following aspects should be considered:

- fair trade
- farming methods
- food safety
- GM food production
- the use of additives in food
- the use of chemicals in food production
- organic production.

Figure 33.1 FAIRTRADE Mark

Many companies now try to follow a code of practice and ensure that products are made in good conditions without exploiting workers. Some of these companies are part of the **Ethical Trading Initiative**.

Fair trade
Revised

The **FAIRTRADE** Mark guarantees that disadvantaged producers are getting a better deal. It means that farmers in developing countries get a fair price for their products, which covers their costs of production.

TRAIDCRAFT
Fighting poverty through trade

Figure 33.2 Traidcraft

It can also help to improve the conditions in which the workers live, e.g. by companies being involved in community projects which improve health and education.

A wide range of Fairtrade products can be purchased.

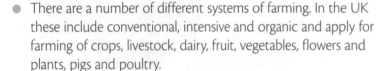

Farming methods
Revised

- There are a number of different systems of farming. In the UK these include conventional, intensive and organic and apply for farming of crops, livestock, dairy, fruit, vegetables, flowers and plants, pigs and poultry.

- Conventional farming techniques use a range of modern technologies to ensure high quantities are produced. Intensive farming makes increased use of resources such as technology and is usually carried out on a large scale to maximise output on as small an area of land as possible. Some people refer to intensive farming as 'factory farming'. There is some debate about animal welfare standards and some believe animals are kept in cramped conditions, with limited lighting and no room for the animals to move or exercise. However, others feel intensive farms operate to very high standards of animal welfare.

Figure 33.3 Free-range hens

- Poultry and eggs can be classed as free range and animals must have access to the outdoors for the majority of their lives. Products from these animals will often cost the consumer more as the animals may have been reared for longer, more land is required and because the yields are lower.

Some people choose to buy food which has been produced to higher standards of animal welfare or environmental protection. They may not want to consume foods they perceive to have been factory farmed.

Figure 33.4 Red Tractor Assurance logo

We all want quality food that is affordable and safe to eat. The Red Tractor is an independent mark of quality that guarantees that the food we are buying comes from farms and food companies that meet high standards of food safety and hygiene, animal welfare and environmental protection. The flag in the Red Tractor logo guarantees the food's origin. The Union Flag provides an independently verified guarantee that the food you're buying has been farmed, processed and packed in the UK. Many food and drink products sold in the UK now have the **Red Tractor Assurance** logo.

Organic food production Revised

All food sold as organic must be approved by organic certification bodies such as the Soil Association which certifies over 70 per cent of all organic product sold in the UK.

- Organic farming systems work with nature, are kind to animals, respect soil structure and help promote wildlife.
- Organic food is produced by farmers who grow, handle and process crops without synthetic fertilisers or herbicides.
- A limited number of naturally derived pesticides are allowed but under very restricted circumstances. The use of sprays in organic systems is closely monitored and controlled and most organic growers use no sprays at all.
- Organic food will not contain any genetically engineered ingredients.
- Only natural fertilisers can be used.
- Choosing processed organic food means avoiding most of the 290 additives allowed in non-organic food, including all artificial colours and flavours. Hydrogenated fats and controversial additives are also banned including aspartame, tartrazine and MSG.
- Organic meat, poultry, eggs and dairy products come from animals that are not given any growth hormones and routine use of antibiotics is banned.
- Many people consider organic foods to taste nicer.
- Organic foods are farmed in a way that is concerned with animal welfare, and the structure and wellbeing of the soil and wildlife.

Figure 33.5 Soil Association logo

> **examiner tip**
> Check regularly for new labels used on food products linked to food production.

Genetically modified (GM) foods Revised

- The genetic make-up of GM foods has been modified or engineered.
- If a product contains over 1 per cent of GM food this must be stated on the label. If the proportion is under 1 per cent it does not need to be stated.
- Currently no GM crops have been authorised to be grown commercially in the UK.

(See also Chapter 36.)

Use of additives Revised

Some consumers choose not to purchase foods containing additives because they think they can affect health and the behaviour of some children. (See also Chapter 16.)

Food preparation

Food manufacturers have a moral and legal obligation to train food workers. They also must ensure food is correctly date marked so that it does not adversely affect consumer's health. (See also Chapter 23.)

Check your understanding Tested

1. Give **three** reasons people may choose to purchase Fairtrade products. (3 marks)
2. Explain what is meant by free-range poultry. (2 marks)
3. State **one** reason some people will not purchase foods containing additives. (1 mark)
4. Give **one** reason some people will not buy Fairtrade products. (1 mark)
5. Explain what is meant by organic food production. (2 marks)

34 Social and cultural influences

Social issues
Revised

Eating habits have been affected by social changes within UK households during the past 30 years, including changes in lifestyle. This has resulted in:

- people spending less time in the kitchen preparing food from raw ingredients
- people choosing to buy more foods that are ready to eat or that just need reheating
- an increase in eating out
- the family eating at different times: some of the traditional mealtimes of breakfast, lunch and dinner are being replaced by snack meals and takeaway dinners.

Other factors that affect eating habits include the following:

- More mothers are employed outside the home.
- More people live alone.
- People travel greater distances to work.
- People have social activities outside the home.
- The use of convenience foods, ready meals and availability of 'takeaways' allow people to have more flexible lifestyles.
- There is a wide variety of foods available to choose from.
- There are many types of restaurants in most urban areas.
- There is less emphasis on the family meal, and family members eat when they want to (grazing).
- Cost is an issue for many people. Some people do not have much money to spend on food. Their choice of food is limited. Other people have more money to spend on food products and there has been an increase in the number of luxury products available.

Figure 34.1 The NHS is spending valuable funds on helping people with diet-related disorders

examiner tip

Keep up to date with changes: read newspaper and magazine articles linked to social and cultural issues in relation to food.

Cultural influences
Revised

A cultural group is a group of people that share the same beliefs and values.

Certain foods have become an important part of celebrations in many cultures, such as:

- special events in the year, e.g. Christmas, Divali
- birthdays
- weddings

- retirements
- special achievements
- to celebrate someone's life.

Every culture in the world has its own type of eating patterns and styles. We adopt the eating patterns of our parents from infancy.

Styles of eating and cooking are determined by the availability of cheap, locally grown food products. Rice is the staple crop in India, China and Japan, the potato in Britain and yams in parts of Africa.

Manufacturers are influenced by cultures – if there is a demand for a certain type of food they will respond.

Religious and moral issues
Revised

Religious beliefs influence eating habits, as religions often have laws related to foods. The main religions that have laws relating to food are:

- Hinduism
- Sikhism
- Islam
- Judaism
- Rastafarianism
- Buddhism.

Check your understanding
Tested

1 State **two** religions that follow a vegetarian diet. (2 marks)
2 Give **three** reasons why eating patterns have changed in the last 30 years. (3 marks)
3 Explain what is meant by a cultural group. (1 mark)
4 State **three** cultural factors that affect people's style of eating. (3 marks)
5 Explain how lack of money may affect a person's choice of food. (2 marks)

35 Environmental issues

More people are stopping to consider the impact that our food has on the environment. When manufacturers consider the impact of a product they look at the 'life-cycle analysis' of the product.

Figure 35.1 Life-cycle analysis

Packaging and the environment

Revised

Food packaging can cause a number of problems because:

- it uses up **natural resources**
- it can cause **pollution**
- it cannot always be recycled and is not always **biodegradable**
- it has to be disposed of in landfill sites.

Consumers can reduce environmental impact by:

- buying re-usable containers and cartons
- reusing carrier bags
- taking waste packaging to recycling centres
- buying products with minimum packaging
- selecting biodegradable materials.

Manufacturers can reduce environmental impact by:

- reducing the amount of packaging
- using paper or card from sustainable forests
- avoiding processes, such as bleaching wood pulp with chemicals
- using materials which the consumer can recycle
- printing symbols on the packaging that inform consumers how to dispose of materials.

Figure 35.2 Recycling logo

Carbon footprint

Revised

An individual's or organisation's carbon footprint is a measure of the impact their activities have on the environment, in terms of the amount of greenhouse gas they produce.

In food technology, the carbon footprint is measured in terms of the following:

- the chemicals involved in the production of the foods
- fuel for machines
- the fuel and energy used in the manufacturing process, including the packaging
- the transportation of the foods
- storage of the food product
- the energy required to dispose of the packaging and food waste.

To reduce your carbon footprint:

- buy fresh local produce
- cook fresh meals
- use local seasonal ingredients
- cut down on your consumption of meat – more energy is used to raise animals than to grow vegetables.

Figure 35.3 Carbon footprint symbol

Food miles

- The distance food travels from field to plate – it is a way of indicating the environmental impact of the food we eat.
- We can reduce food miles by buying locally produced products.

Energy

- The consumption of **non-renewable energy resources** such as coal and oil is causing an energy crisis. These resources will eventually run out.
- Using non-renewable resources adds to the pollution problem.
- **Green energy** is obtained from alternative energy sources.

Figure 35.4 Wind turbines

Ways in which you can reduce your energy consumption include the following:

- Never put the oven on for just one food product.
- Use a steamer with several vegetables cooking at once.
- Use a pressure cooker to cook stews in 20 minutes or whole meals very quickly.
- Use a microwave to quickly cook products.
- Turn the heat down and use a lid on pans.
- Stir fry as a quick method of cooking.
- Use hand skills of chopping, grating, shredding, whisking instead of using electrical equipment.
- Try to make 'one pan' recipes.

Check your understanding

Tested

1 State **three** ways consumers can reduce their energy consumption when cooking food. (3 marks)
2 State **three** ways manufacturers could reduce the impact their packaging has on the environment. (3 marks)
3 Describe what is meant by 'non-renewable energy sources'. (2 marks)
4 Explain what is meant by 'carbon footprint'. (2 marks)
5 Explain how consumers can reduce the amount of waste going to landfill sites. (4 marks)

Technological developments

36 Technological developments

Genetically modified (GM) foods

Genetically modified (GM) is the term used to refer to crops of which the genetic structure has been changed.

Figure 36.1 Genetically modified crop

Advantages:

- Can improve the quality of food, e.g. food will stay fresh for longer.
- Can grow in difficult conditions.
- Herbicide and insect resistant.
- Have higher nutritional value.
- Can be cheaper to produce.

Concerns:

- Long-term safety is unknown.
- Environmental issues, e.g. how crops might be affected.
- Lack of communication between provider and consumer.
- Lack of clear labelling.

> **examiner's tip**
>
> If a question asks for advantages and disadvantages you must answer the question from both points of view. Do not give opposites.

Modified starches

Modified starches are used to improve the quality of foods. They are used in a wide range of foods and can be used for different purposes, e.g.

- to prevents sauces splitting, e.g. in ready meals
- to instantly thicken products, e.g. in pot noodles
- as a cold gelling agent – cold liquid is added and the mixture thickens
- to stop emulsions separating, e.g. in salad dressings.

Functional foods

These have extra health benefits above their basic nutritional value. Supermarkets promote these as 'functional foods' because they contribute to good health.

- Examples of functional foods include probiotic foods, prebiotic foods and plant sterols and stanols.

Nanotechnology

Nanotechnology is one of the latest trends in food technology. It means working with materials at a microscopic level.
It includes:

- nano-emulsions, which improve the texture of sauces
- nano-food synthesisers, which can create or alter food molecules
- nano-capsule protection, which can add a fortifying nutrient to our body that is then slowly released; or can release a controlled flavour into a drink

- nano-sensors, which record the changes in pH, temperature or the presence of pathogens
- nano-bots, which are microbe-destroying, minute robots that can make food safe.

Food trends

Revised

Food trends change over time. Recent trends have included:
- an increase in the development of authentic ethnic foods
- more sandwiches being sold in shops
- traditional food products becoming more popular, e.g. steamed puddings
- healthy eating claims on foods
- an increase in the variety of vegetable dishes
- more new products that are targeted at children, e.g. breakfast bars
- organic foods
- an increase in products suitable for vegetarians and other special diets.

What are the trends for the future?

Revised

Predictions include:
- more products that can be cooked by microwave
- demand for healthier foods and organic ingredients
- greater demand for single portions
- nostalgia products, products from the past that look and taste more 'homemade'
- eco-friendly packaging
- increased consumption of locally produced sustainable foods
- healthy ready-meals that are targeted at children
- innovative low-calorie products for weight watchers
- foods that can fight diseases
- more indulgent foods, such as luxury desserts
- less meat and a rise in the consumption of fruits, vegetables and whole grains
- useful bacteria to gain entry into many other food items
- more snacking for busy people who cannot stop for food
- increased consumption of raw food in the form of salads.

Check your understanding

Tested

1 Give **two** advantages and two disadvantages of genetically modified foods. (4 marks)
2 State what is meant by functional foods. (1 mark)
3 Give **two** reasons why there has been an increase in the sales of functional foods. (2 marks)
4 Explain why there has been a trend for food manufacturers to state nutritional claims on product labelling. (4 marks)
5 It is predicted that there will be an increase in the sales of locally and sustainably produced foods. Give *three* reasons for this. (3 marks)

Answers to 'Check your understanding' questions

Where a range of possible answers are given, you can have a selection from any of those listed and get the total marks available (e.g. for a four-mark question you only need four answers from the list; you do not have to list all the options given to get the available marks). In some cases, other answers not listed would also be correct. Check in your textbook to make sure any answers you have given that are not listed are suitable.

1 A balanced diet

1 Obesity, coronary heart disease (CHD), strokes, Type 2 diabetes, some cancers. (2 marks)
2 Sandwich with wholemeal bread, polyunsaturated margarine, ham and tomato; chopped fresh vegetables (cucumber, carrots and peppers); fresh orange juice, water or milk; fresh fruit (e.g. apple) and/or yoghurt. (4 marks)
3 It causes high blood pressure. (1 mark)
4 Herbs, spices, garlic, pepper. (2 marks)
5 PE lessons; after-school sports clubs; water fountains; water bottles in lessons; PSHE; Food Technology lessons on healthy eating, including the Eatwell plate; cooking clubs; school meals improved; more fresh fruit available; award systems for a healthier lunch choice; Jamie Oliver's influence; no fizzy drinks machines/ vending machines; five a day campaign; breakfast clubs; cycling; walking to school. (6 marks)

2 Protein

1 Body building; repair of cells; formation of hormones or enzymes; energy. (3 marks)
2 Proteins that cannot be made by the body. (1 mark)
3 Soya or Quorn®. (1 mark)
4 Lentil curry and rice; vegetable lasagne; nut roast. (2 marks)
5 Toddler: milk; lacto-vegetarian: milk, eggs or cheese; elderly person: fish or meat. (3 marks)

3 Fats and oils

1 Concentrated source of energy; structure of cells; insulate the body; protect vital organs; fat-soluble vitamins A, D, E and K; essential fatty acids; gives foods texture and flavour; feeling of satiety. (4 marks)
2 Easy to swallow; look appealing; glossy or crispy appearance. (2 marks)
3 Linked to high blood cholesterol; leading to an increased risk of coronary heart disease; diabetes; obesity. (4 marks)
4 Excess fat consumed is stored as fat. (1 mark)
5 Cholesterol, a type of saturated fat produced in the liver, is deposited on the walls of the arteries, narrowing them. Narrowed arteries are one of the major causes of coronary heart disease. (4 marks)

4 Carbohydrate

1 Provides the body with energy; energy to maintain bodily functions; provide dietary fibre (non-starch polysaccharide (NSP); to help digestion; sweeten and flavour foods. (3 marks)
2 Intrinsic sugar is part of the cells and does not react with plaque. Extrinsic sugars, e.g. cane sugar/sucrose reacts with the bacteria in the mouth (plaque) and produces an acid. Acid then causes holes in teeth. Plaque + sucrose = acid. Acid + tooth = decay. (4 marks)
3 To prevent constipation; add bulk to increase waste matter; to reduce cholesterol levels; prevent bowel disorders. (2 marks)
4 Wholemeal bread; beans; lentils; nuts; wholemeal pasta; brown rice; jacket potato; fruits; vegetables. (2 marks)
5 Constipation; diverticular disease; bowel cancer; appendicitis; haemorrhoids. (2 marks)

5 Vitamins, minerals and water

1 a. Calcium; phosphorus; vitamin D
   b. Iron
   c. Vitamin A
   d. Vitamin B
   e. Vitamin C (5 marks)
2 Vitamin D (1 mark)
3 Vitamin A and D (2 marks)
4 a. Calcium
   b. Iron
   c. Sodium
   d. Fluoride (4 marks)
5 Helps regulate the body's temperature (cools us/ prevents heat stroke); helps the kidneys flush out harmful substances; transports nutrients, oxygen and carbon dioxide round the body; for all body processes (e.g. digestion); prevents dehydration. (4 marks)

6 Cereals

1 How much of the whole grain is used; different flours have different extraction rates (e.g. wholemeal 100 per cent, brown flour 85–95 per cent, white flour 55–70 per cent). (2 marks)
2 Food that is cheaper to produce in a country in comparison to protein, e.g. rice in China. (2 marks)
3 Calcium; iron; niacin; thiamine. (4 marks)

4 Long grain; short grain; frozen; cook chill; canned; quick; fast cook; boil in the bag. (3 marks)

5 Good source of carbohydrate for energy; low in fat; contain protein – LBV – growth, repair, maintenance; if wholegrain – good fibre content; wide variety – gives choice; products developing all the time, e.g. Oatly® milk for lactose-intolerant consumers. (4 marks)

7 Fruits and vegetables

1 Fruits: blackcurrants, rosehips, citrus fruits, strawberries, gooseberries, raspberries, oranges. (2 marks)

2 Vegetables: sprouts, cabbage, green peppers, spinach, watercress, peas, bean sprouts, potatoes. (3 marks)

3 Prepare vegetables just before cooking to prevent loss of vitamins by the action of enzymes and oxidisation. Do not soak them in water to prevent the loss of water-soluble vitamins. Steam the vegetables to prevent water-soluble vitamins being lost into cooking water. Use as little water as possible. Cut into small pieces so they cook quickly. (4 marks)

4 Contains fibre – prevents constipation; reduces bowel cancer; reduces diverticular disease. Naturally low in fat – reduces fat intake; reducing heart disease; obesity. Filling – but are low in calories. Vitamin C – green vegetables – formation of connective tissue; helps absorption of calcium; healing wounds; absorption of iron; scurvy. Vitamin A (carotene) – carrots; keeps eyes healthy; improves night vision; helps maintain skin/mucous membranes. Minerals: potassium – bananas; help muscles and nerve function; helps to reduce blood pressure. Iron – from dark green vegetables and pulses; prevents anaemia; formation of haemoglobin/red blood cells; transporting of oxygen; maintains cell functions. High in antioxidants – cancer-fighting benefits; lycopene. (4 marks)

5 Peas, beans and lentils. (3 marks)

8 Meat and fish

1 The fibres are much shorter and the connective tissue is much finer; therefore it does not take long to cook. (2 marks)

2 Cross-contamination – can cause food poisoning. Cover and store the meat at the bottom of the fridge so that it cannot touch any other foods. Raw meat contains harmful bacteria that can spread to anything it touches. Smell of fish can pass to other products – spoiling the flavour. (4 marks)

3 Protein, fat, B vitamins, iron, water, vitamin A. (6 marks)

4 Does not contain a lot of fat – linked to health reasons, e.g. CHD; obesity; good source of protein; growth; repair. Oily fish contains essential fatty acids. (4 marks)

5 Keep raw meat separate from other foods. Cover and store at the bottom of the fridge. Store at temperatures below 5°C. (3 marks)

9 Dairy products and eggs

1 UHT; pasteurised; sterilised; condensed; dried. (3 marks)

2 Reduced fat content; reduced amount of saturated fat. Too much fat in the diet is linked to heart disease, cholesterol and high blood pressure. (2 marks)

3 Protein; fat; calcium; vitamin A; vitamin D; small amount thiamin; riboflavin. (3 marks)

4 Source of protein, B vitamins, fat, vitamin A, iron. Can be used to make a variety of different dishes (main course dishes and desserts). Relatively cheap source of protein. Good source of protein for ovo-lacto vegetarians. (4 marks)

5 Fridge (0–5°C) – slows down growth of bacteria. (2 marks)

10 Fats and oils

1 Fat; vitamin A; vitamin D. (2 marks)

2 Contain less saturated fat – linked to CHD and high cholesterol. Variety of different fats available; often low fat spreads. Publicity about reducing saturated/animal fats. (4 marks)

3 Vegetable – olive, corn, rapeseed; animal – butter, lard, suet. (4 marks)

4 High percentage of water – means they do not mix correctly, when heated the spread separates because of the high water content. (2 marks)

5 Margarine. (1 mark)

11 Alternative protein foods

1 Contains egg white – vegans do not eat any product from animals. (2 marks)

2 Contain all essential amino acids – high biological value protein foods. (2 marks)

3 Tofu; soya milk; soya mince (tinned, frozen, dried); soya products such as burgers and sausages. (2 marks)

4 Any named herb; spice; onions; garlic; chilli; soya; Worcester sauce etc. (3 marks)

5 Any named soya product; Quorn®. (2 marks)

12 Diet and food choice

1 Heath issues; medical advice; fashion; religion; moral rights; do not like meat; cost of meat; avoiding animal fats. (4 marks)

2 Vegan – no products from an animal; lacto-ovo vegetarian – will eat animal products but not any that involves killing an animal. (2 marks)

3 TVP; tofu; nuts; pulses; peas; lentils; vegetarian sausages; rice; seeds; sauce with soya milk. (3 marks)

4 Peer pressure; time available; money; sport or leisure activity; family influence; personal likes; culture. (4 marks)

5 Wider range available; busy lifestyles; eating at different times; better quality; advertising; less washing up; improved taste; 'healthy option' ranges available. (3 marks)

13 Special diets

1 Eat more fruits and vegetables; take regular physical exercise; do not smoke; eat a varied diet; cut back on the fat in your diet and cooking; eat more starchy carbohydrate; use monounsaturated fats (olive oil); have fish instead of meat. (4 marks)

2 Smoking; high blood pressure; raised levels of cholesterol; obesity; a family history; low levels of exercise. (4 marks)

3 Rice; potatoes; quinoa; buckwheat. (4 marks)

4 Soya milk; oat milk. (1 mark)

5 Calcium for bones and teeth in baby. Mother would lose her own supply to baby if extra not supplied in diet. Iron for baby's blood – it has to last until the baby is six months old. (4 marks)

14 Energy balance

1 The relationship between food intake and energy used. (2 marks)

2 To give guidance to people to eat a balanced amount; help to reduce obesity; so that consumers know the amount of energy in the food products that they buy. (2 marks)

3 Do more physical exercise. (1 mark)

4 Stored as body fat. (1 mark)

5 Age; body size; gender; activity level; state of body (illness/pregnancy); occupation; time of year. (5 marks)

15 Functions of ingredients

1

Ingredient	Function
Pastry base	
Flour	Adds bulk, provides the main structure
Fat	Adds flavour, helps extend shelf life, shortens, adds moisture
Water	Binds ingredients together, adds moisture
Filling and topping	
Lemon	Adds flavour, provides vitamin C
Eggs	Aids setting/coagulation, aerates, provides colour, provides protein
Cornflour	Setting/thickening
Sugar	Sweetens, adds flavour

(7 marks)

2 a) Raising agent; makes bread rise; flavour; to provide carbon dioxide.

b) Provides bulk; provides gluten – holds bread in risen shape. (2 marks)

3 Food; warmth; moisture; time. (2 marks)

4 a) Cocoa; chocolate; coffee; vanilla essence; lemon or orange juice; rind; suitable fruit flavours; spices. (2 marks)

b) Chopped cherries; coconut; dried fruit; chocolate chips; wholemeal flour; nuts; oats; fresh fruit. (1 mark)

c) Colour; caramelisation; sweeten; flavour; preserve; increase shelf life; hold or trap air. (1 mark)

16 Additives and food components

1 a) Protect against growth of micro-organisms; increase shelf life.

b) Prevent fat combining with oxygen and becoming rancid – spoiling taste and giving unpleasant smell; slows down enzyme activity in fruits and vegetables that go brown when cut.

c) Help oil and water mix together; give foods a smooth creamy texture, e.g. desserts. (3 marks)

2 Can be used in a wide range of products; improve specific characteristics; produce expected qualities; allow a product range, e.g. different flavoured crisps; maintain product consistency in large-scale production; restore original characteristics after processing food; prevent spoilage and gives a longer shelf life; disguise inferior ingredients so reducing costs. (4 marks)

3 Some people may have an allergy to additives. (1 mark)

4 Process whereby foods have nutrients added to increase their nutritional value. These are described as 'fortified' foods. (2 marks)

5 Saves preparation time; cuts cost as specialised equipment required to make decorations would not have to be bought; same results every time; high quality products, quality guaranteed; less manpower needed; ready immediately when needed. (2 marks)

17 Methods of cooking and heat transference

1 Very little fat or oil is used, therefore fat content in product is lower. Quick method of cooking – less loss of nutrients. Water-soluble vitamins not lost. (2 marks)

2 Use a microwave. Do not put the oven on for just one dish/fill oven. Cook in bulk and then freeze foods. Use of a pressure cooker – whole meals/stews. When boiling foods keep a lid on the pan and use as little liquid as possible for boiling. Use a kettle to boil water for vegetables/rice/pasta. Use the correct size pan for the size of the hob/control level of heat under pan. Use of slow cookers or slow cooker setting on cookers. Use of stir-frying as a very quick method of cooking. Family eats together so oven is only used once. Cook some vegetables together in same pan rather than separately/one-pot meals. (6 marks)

3 Microwaves entering the food and causing the molecules of water in the food to vibrate. The friction produces the heat. (3 marks)

4 Conduction, convection, radiation. (3 marks)

5 Advantages – A quick method of cooking; no added fat; reduces the fat content of foods, e.g. sausages.

Disadvantages – Not suitable for tough cuts of meat; careful timing of cooking is needed so foods are not overcooked. (4 marks)

18 The effect of heat on different foods

1 Coagulate or set – if overheated they become tough/difficult to digest; synerisis occurs. (2 marks)

2 Starch grains are mixed into the liquid but not able to dissolve in cold liquid. Liquid is heated, the starch grains swell. More heat is applied, the starch grains break open, causing the mixture to thicken (gelatinisation). (3 marks)

3 To make them digestible. (1 mark)

4 Melts and becomes syrup – at 154°C the sugar starts to change colour (caramelisation). (2 marks)

5 Add to boiling water. Steam. Cook for as little time as possible. Use as little water as possible. Cut into small pieces so they cook quickly. (3 marks)

19 Tools and equipment

1 Point down and away when cutting; hold by handle, keep fingers away from blade; correct knife for the job; keep sharpened; no chips in blade; hands, handles not greasy; cut on a stable surface, e.g. chopping board; store correctly, e.g. knife block, drawer (all facing same direction); wash after use to prevent contamination; care when washing. (2 marks)

2 Chopping; breaking down food; cutting into small pieces; making breadcrumbs; pureeing; blending; liquidising; making milkshake; soup; mixing; creaming; rubbing in; slicing; grating; dicing. (2 marks)

3 Blue. (1 mark)

4 Complete tasks safely, hygienically and efficiently; achieve a consistency of finish; achieve a quality outcome. (1 mark)

5 Indicates that the required safety standards have been met on large-scale industrial equipment. (2 marks)

20 Food spoilage and storage

1

Food	Where it should be stored	Why it is stored in this place
Fresh fruit salad	Fridge Chiller	Maintains texture/taste Lasts longer Keeps it fresh Slows down growth of micro-organisms/yeasts/bacteria/moulds (2 marks)
Ice cream	Freezer	Remains frozen Bacteria are dormant (2 marks)

2 Meat; fish; eggs; milk; cheese; ready prepared foods; cream; gravy; custard; cooked rice. (1 mark)

3 Pathogenic bacteria; salmonella; E. coli; staphylococcus; listeria; botulinum; campylobacter. (1 mark)

4 Temperature is too low for bacteria to multiply; water is not available. (1 mark)

5 Foods with a high water content are not suitable for freezing; the water freezes into crystals, which burst the cell walls; when it thaws the cells collapse. (2 marks)

21 Preservation and extending shelf life

1 Any temperature between 0 and 8°C. (1 mark)

2 To make sure it is within the legal limits; make sure it is not above 8°C; make sure it is not too cold, causing food to freeze; not too warm, so food is in good condition, fresh; to make sure it is working; it is a legal requirement. (2 marks)

3 Requires no defrosting; nutritional value retained; can have a good quality appearance, colour, flavour, texture, tastes fresh; available in single portions, suitable for people living on their own; can be frozen; no skill required, easy to prepare, cook; consistent quality; little equipment needed; suitable for people with busy lifestyles; wide variety available; little waste. (3 marks)

4 Cold temperature does not destroy the bacteria, they become dormant, cannot multiply; bacteria need moisture to multiply – water becomes unavailable for the bacteria to reproduce as it forms ice crystals; enzyme activity in the food is slowed down because of the cold temperatures. (2 marks)

5 Important in planning distribution of products; if the product only has a short shelf life it limits the amount of selling time and money could be lost; retailers often want products with a long shelf life to maintain profits so need to be confident the product is sold in good condition; can identify when the product will begin to deteriorate so they will not receive complaints about low standard products and therefore bad press; so they feel confident they are not selling products that may cause food poisoning. (2 marks)

22 Packaging of food products

1 a) Strong; lightweight; flexible; does not react with food; barrier to moisture; can be printed; can be vacuum formed; can be frozen; waterproof; microwaveable; cheap (to produce); can be recycled; can be coloured; can be made see-through.

b) Can be recycled; strong; rigid; barrier to moisture; can be printed; different thicknesses; can be laminated; no special storage needed; keep fresh.

c) Renewable source; can be recycled; easily printed; strong; lightweight; variety of shapes and sizes; if treated can hold liquids; microwaveable; different thicknesses; cheap to produce; easy to open; keep fresh; biodegradable. (3 marks)

2 Protects (food from damage); increases shelf life; gives information; protects from contamination; easy to store; allows you to stack; to promote; keeps together, e.g. small pieces; stops leakage; container to eat from; container to cook in; keeps out moisture;

stops product drying out; keeps product in shape; tamperproof. (2 marks)

3   a) Box; tray; (pickled eggs) jar

b) Paper bag; plastic; netting; can; tin; plastic bag

c) Carton; bottle; tetra pack. (3 marks)

4   Use of bright colours; use of bold writing; interesting serving suggestions; clear pictures of the product, adding pictures; celebrities endorsing the product; events endorsing the product; use of interesting, different fonts, fancy writing; being able to view the product; promotions; interesting shape. (2 marks)

5   To see if the packaging has been opened, so reducing the risk of the food becoming contaminated. (1 mark)

23 Labelling of food products

1   Food product name; address of manufacturer; name of manufacturer; storage conditions required; shelf life – 'use by' date, 'best before' date; instructions for use; cooking instructions; place of origin; weight or volume; description of food product; allergies. (3 marks)

2   Shows the price at the checkout when barcode scanned; details used for stock taking; see what people are buying; automatic reordering; quicker response at the till; allows customers to check prices on scanners in some shops; allows customers to do self-service shopping. (1 mark)

3   Consumer knows what nutrients are in the product; allows the consumer to compare products; consumers can make informed choices if on a special diet, e.g. low fat, low sugar; foods that have specific nutrient content can be purchased to meet the consumer's needs; compare with guidelines for daily amount. (2 marks)

4   Protects from contamination in transit from other foods, dirt, cross-contamination; correct choice of material to suit cooking, storage; correctly sealed, e.g. microwave meals; using impermeable materials so airtight – bacteria cannot enter; avoids cross-contamination, e.g. vacuum packing, canning, UHT; use of packaging systems to exchange air for gases – MAP; vacuum packing – bacteria have no access to oxygen; packaging by heat treatment – have a long shelf life because all bacteria are destroyed, e.g. UHT; packaging materials extend shelf life, e.g. glass. (4 marks)

5   List of ingredients – identifies high-risk foods; correct storage information given, e.g. chilled foods below 8°C to reduce bacterial growth; date marking to inform customers about correct length of time that food should be stored; warnings, e.g. not suitable for freezing; chilled foods that have previously been frozen. (4 marks)

24 Hygiene practices

1   Bacteria are transferred/passed from one food to another, from raw to cooked; bacteria are carried on a knife/chopping board from one food to another. (1 mark)

2   Pathogenic. (1 mark)

3   Raw and cooked foods should not touch each other; blood and juices of raw foods should not drip onto cooked foods; preparation in separate areas; use

different coloured chopping boards, knives etc.; washing hands and work surface between tasks. (3 marks)

4   Correct temperature to control bacterial growth; preventing products from getting squashed or damaged, stack safely; prevent contact with chemicals, cleaning products, which might contaminate; should be as fast as possible, to prevent bacterial growth; correct size vehicle to make it cost effective; check seals to avoid contamination; protective packaging – secondary packaging to avoid contamination; clear labelling to ensure correct delivery; instruction to handlers, e.g. 'store this way up' to prevent damage; staff training to reduce accidents; contamination; checking stock on/off vehicle; batch numbers; pest/vermin control to prevent contamination; efficient system so stock delivered on time to ensure quality. (4 marks)

5   Incorrect storage of food products so bacteria grow; cross-contamination; those preparing food not following correct hygiene procedures, e.g. not washing hands; poor preparation – cross-contamination by incorrect use of equipment; prepared too far in advance; incorrect cooking procedures – insufficient time, incorrect temperature, not kept above 63°C if hot holding; not following date marking, particularly for high risk foods; increased use of microwaves – food not always defrosted or cooked/reheated correctly; more people eating out; increased use of cook-chill and frozen products. (3 marks)

25 Risk assessment and environmental health

1   Making an assessment of any risk to a food product during its production and to take the required action to ensure the safety of the food. (2 marks)

2   Hazard Analysis Critical Control Point. (1 mark)

3   Showing and proving that all reasonable precautions have been taken to prevent an offence arising. (1 mark)

4   Enforce the Food Safety Act, legislation; investigate food poisoning outbreaks; give advice on safe food preparation; monitor working conditions and hygiene systems; inspect food premises regularly; suggest improvements; aim to reduce possible sources of cross-contamination; run food hygiene courses; ensure food is fit for human consumption; close down unfit food premises; inspect food at ports/slaughter houses to see that it is safe to eat; remove food samples for testing; prosecute employers and employees. (4 marks)

5   The steps in the making process where high-risk hazards (e.g. micro-biological) must be controlled because they could result in food poisoning. (2 marks)

26 Food safety

1   Environmental Health Officers and the Trading Standards Office. (1 mark)

2 Hair covered with hat or net or hair tied back; covered cuts with blue plaster; no jewellery; protective clothing worn (e.g. apron or overall); wash hands before starting work and after going to the toilet; don't cough or sneeze over food; wear gloves; nails cut short, clean and with no nail varnish. (3 marks)

3 To prevent cross-contamination. (2 marks)

4 72°C or higher. (1 mark)

5 Ensures all food is safe to eat; ensures high standards of hygiene, including preparation, supply and sale; staff training; prevents sale of food which may be harmful to health or cause food poisoning; prevents contamination of food by pieces of metal, pests, chemicals etc.; makes sure all food products match descriptions or claims made about them; requires the food industry to assess risks involved in food production; setting up HACCP procedures; requires high-risk food is kept at temperatures below 8°C or reheated food is served hot at above 63°C; describes the information that should be on a food label; microbiological sampling; premises inspected regularly; legislation enforced by EHO or Trading Standards Officer; food must be safely prepared, processed, manufactured, packaged, transported, distributed and sold. (5 marks)

27 CAD, CAM, quality assurance and quality control

1 Creating questionnaires; analysing results of questionnaires; product reports to the retailer; using internet to research existing products; emailing questionnaires; nutritional analysis; calculating costs; sensory analysis; scaling up of ingredients; producing packaging nets; labelling. (2 marks)

2 Greater accuracy, e.g. working out nutritional analysis; professional finish, e.g. graphics/artwork on packaging; tasks can be completed quickly, e.g. annotated drawings; graphical work for packaging; colours and graphic effects can be modelled and tried out; designs can easily be varied when product changes; modelling of recipes without wasting money trialling products. (2 marks)

3 'A level of guarantee' or 'positive declaration'. (1 mark)

4 Visual checks; using cutters or slicers; using depositors ensures same amount of filling; thermostatically controlled ovens; use of pie presses, moulds, same size tins; accurate weighing; rolling pastry to the same thickness; temperature control during cooking process; time control during cooking process. (3 marks)

5 a) Ensures consistency for every batch; eliminates human error; each biscuit is identical every time.

b) Controls conveyor belt speed through ovens; maintains even/correct temperature in ovens; cooked for the same time; ensures even colour; not overcooked or undercooked.

c) Deposits accurate amount of chocolate; ensures even thickness of chocolate across biscuit; consistent appearance in each batch. (3 marks)

28 Commercial production methods

1 Can bulk buy ingredients, saving money; reduces overall costs of products; products can be made in specific amounts, small amounts, to order; recipes can be varied easily, e.g. changing flavour; equipment can be used to make other products; staff have job satisfaction – more interesting work for staff; products can be easily modified e.g. to meet changes in consumer demand, e.g. easier to alter number in batch to meet changes from client; less likely to have errors; all same quality; accurate – no mistakes, identical product; quicker than handmade; fast to produce large number of products. (2 marks)

2 Few staff needed; inexpensive to run; equipment used all of time; more efficient as can be used for range of products, non-stop for 24 hours a day; lots of products can be made – no setting up time required, so costs reduced; repetition of skills so some staff can be less skilled/less training needed. (1 mark)

3 Expensive to set up; important to keep the machinery in good working order, to keep the plant running; dedicated to one process only. Cannot be adapted to meet customer needs; if goes wrong, can be very expensive; very wasteful; if there is a breakdown in any machinery then all production stops. (1 mark)

4 Individual; unique; high quality. (2 marks)

5 Can take a long time to manufacture as processes are carried out by hand; can be expensive. (2 marks)

29 Design process

1 Talk to supermarket staff; look at existing products; questionnaire; survey; internet. (2 marks)

2 Surveys, questionnaires, asking people; looking at/ evaluating existing products; looking at recipes books; using internet. (1 mark)

3 Qualities can be monitored and improvements identified so the product is being developed according to users' views. Money is therefore not wasted, as products will be what consumers want. (2 marks)

4 Design specification – gives general criteria; Product specification – describes very specific characteristics. (2 marks)

5

Design specification	Ingredient
Colourful	Contrast of two colours Colourful ingredients, e.g. red and green peppers Sauce, e.g. cheese, tomato, curry Specified pasta colour Bread crumbs/cheese on the top – browning
To have a variety of textures	State two foods and their textures Sauce – smooth Vegetables – may give specific vegetable – crunchy Pasta – chewy Meat – chewy/soft Fish – chewy/soft

To be high in fibre	Wholemeal pasta, wholemeal breadcrumbs, vegetables Ingredient that contains high amount of fibre, e.g. wholemeal pasta instead of refined pasta Seeds, nuts, pulses/peas/beans/lentils, dried fruit, fruit
Contains protein	Meat, fish, eggs, cheese, Quorn® products, peas, beans, lentils, poultry, tofu, nuts

(4 marks)

30 Sensory analysis

1 Check that the product matches the specification; match the product against competitors' products; identify areas for improvement; determine whether the consumer likes it; find out what the consumer wants; test shelf-life; check standards throughout production. (2 marks)

2 Rating test – involves giving food products a score; usually scores out of 5; can involve giving a score for a final product or different aspects of the product.

3 Ranking test – putting the products in order of preference; which they liked the most. (2 marks)

4 Three samples are given with two being identical and the third slightly different. Tester is asked to identify the 'odd one out'.

a) Cheese; herbs. (2 marks)

b) Use a stronger cheese, mature cheddar, parmesan; use a herb with a stronger flavour. (1 mark)

c) Star diagram; written report; spreadsheet. (1 mark)

31 Product analysis

1 a) Teenagers; children; workers of any type; holidays; picnic; travel; school lunches; older people; students. (2 marks)

b) Change white bread to wholemeal or high-fibre white; add any named vegetable, e.g. tomatoes, cucumber; change cheese to Quorn®/TVP; add nuts; add any named fruit; use humus. (2 marks)

c) Protect from damage; increase shelf life; give information; transport easily from factory to shop, shop to home; handle easily; protect from contamination; easy to store/stack; keeps the sandwiches compact/together; container to eat from; keeps sandwiches fresh/moist; stops drying out; keeps shape of sandwiches; improves presentation; promotion; advertises product. (2 marks)

2 a) Children; older people. (1 mark)

b) Children: easy to hold; attractive appearance; small portion; suitable for lunch boxes; parents will buy it because of milk content; contains calcium.

Older people: single portion; no preparation; attractive appearance; contains calcium. (2 marks)

c) In a refrigerator; below 8°C; between 1 and 8°C.

3 UHT; long life; pasteurized; sterilised; canned; evaporated; condensed. (2 marks)

4 Cartoon characters on the packaging; attractive packaging; free gifts; advertising on TV/radio; posters; magazines; internet; in-store promotions; samples to try; leaflets; use of famous people; linked to sports; films. (2 marks)

32 The six Rs

1 Primary recycling; secondary or physical recycling; tertiary or chemical recycling. (3 marks)

2 Cost of energy is constantly rising. Most of the energy used in the UK comes from unsustainable sources (e.g. oil, coal, gas). (2 marks)

3 Fat – to reduce/prevent CHD, heart disease or angina, which can be fatal; affects quality of life; restricts blood flow; narrows arteries; to reduce/prevent obesity or being overweight – linked to strain on organs of the body; heart disease; high blood pressure; diabetes; osteoarthritis; varicose veins; breathlessness and chest infections; low self-esteem; to reduce cholesterol levels – restricts blood flow/narrows arteries.

Sugar – to reduce/prevent diabetes – reference to blood sugar levels, poor circulation and/or blindness; to reduce/prevent obesity or being overweight – linked to strain on organs of the body; heart disease; high blood pressure; diabetes; osteoarthritis; varicose veins; breathlessness and chest infections; low self-esteem; tooth decay – bacteria/plaque feed on the sugar to produce acid = tooth decay; recommended that sugars should not provide more than 10 per cent of energy intake – stored as fat if not used for energy.

Salt – to reduce risk of heart disease/stroke; reduce high blood pressure; kidney damage; demineralisation of bones. (6 marks)

4 Discarded packaging creates waste and often ends up in landfill sites – production of gases/pollution; packaging that is recycled uses a lot of energy to recycle – this energy is often from unsustainable sources. (4 marks)

5 Correct storage of foods before using; reference to storing in fridge – below 5°C; specific examples of storing food, e.g. bread in box; correct reheating of foods – to above 75°C; only reheat foods once. (4 marks)

33 Moral issues

1 Supporting other people – fair wages being paid to workers; supporting community, e.g. health projects/ education; range of high quality foods; wide variety of foods. (3 marks)

2 Allowed to roam freely; have access to outdoor and indoor spaces; considered to be a better way for poultry to live. (2 marks)

3 Links to hyperactivity in children; allergic reactions. (1 mark)

4 Cost; amount of food miles – all imported; want to support local growers in UK, not farmers abroad. (1 mark)

5 No synthetic fertilisers, pesticides and herbicides or any other artificial ingredient used; no GM foods/products used; meat/poultry not given antibiotics/growth hormones; is certified by organic certification bodies. (2 marks)

34 Social and cultural influences

1 Buddhism; Islam; Hinduism; Sikhism. (2 marks)

2 Less time spent preparing; increase in ready meals; eating out; different family commitments; more working women; more people live alone; people travel greater distances to work; wide variety of convenience foods; variety of foods available; less emphasis on family meal times. (3 marks)

3 People who share the same beliefs, faith and values. (1 mark)

4 Religion; styles of foods; staple foods; celebrations associated with that culture. (3 marks)

5 Limits choice; cannot always purchase higher nutritional value foods. (2 marks)

35 Environmental issues

1 Oven on for just one dish; use a steamer/cook several vegetables at once; use a pressure cooker/microwave; turn the heat down on hob; put lids on pans; stir-fry as a quick method of cooking; use hand skills instead of using electrical equipment. (3 marks)

2 Reduce the amount of packaging; use paper or card from sustainable forests; avoid processes that use chemicals; use materials that consumer can recycle; put symbols on packaging; use recycled materials. (3 marks)

3 Resources that will eventually run out/cannot be made again once they have all been used, such as oil, coal and gas. (2 marks)

4 A measure of the impact that an individual's or organisation's activities have on the environment in terms of the amount of greenhouse gases produced. Processes right through food production, from the growing of foods through the manufacturing process to the disposal of the product. (2 marks)

5 Packaging: choose products with minimal packaging and/or biodegradable, reusable containers; reuse carrier bags; take waste packaging to recycling centres; reduce food waste; only cook/buy what is needed; check and use food before 'use by' date; compost as much as possible. (4 marks)

36 Technological developments

1 Advantages: Can improve the quality of food, e.g. food will stay fresh for longer; can grow in difficult conditions; herbicide and insect resistant; may have higher nutritional value; can be cheaper to produce. (2 marks)

Disadvantages: Long-term safety is unknown; environmental issues, e.g. how other crops might be affected; lack of communication between provider and consumer; lack of clear labelling on food products. (2 marks)

2 Foods that have extra health benefits above their basic nutritional values. (1 mark)

3 Heavily promoted by manufacturers; increased publicity in media; consumers' awareness of health benefits. (2 marks)

4 Consumers can make informed choices/compare products; check which nutrients are in the product; check for specific nutrients; check daily guidelines; can be used to help plan a balanced diet; explanation of balanced diet; to be able to relate the product to their nutritional/dietary requirements. (4 marks)

5 Less air or food miles; carbon footprint; global warming; carbon emissions/CO_2; cheaper because of the cost of transport/storage; supports local industry/farming; 'Buy British' campaigns; may have a better nutritional profile as will get from the field to the shop in less time – therefore less loss of nutrients; fresher products – may not have been stored for so long/better flavour and texture. (3 marks)

Glossary

Additives – substances which are added to foods during manufacturing or processing to improve their keeping qualities, flavour, colour, texture, appearance, stability

Aerating – process of adding air

Amino acids – the smallest units of a protein

Anaerobic – no oxygen

Anaphylactic reaction – an extreme reaction to a substance needing immediate medical treatment

Aseptic – filling a sterilised pouch with a sterile food in a hygienic environment; giving a product an extended shelf life without the use of preservatives or refrigeration

Balanced diet – a diet that provides the correct amounts of nutrients and energy for optimum growth and health

Basal metabolic rate – the amount of energy we consume for all bodily functions

Batch production – production method used for small numbers of identical or similar products

Biodegradable – material broken down totally by bacteria

Blanch – plunge cut vegetables into hot water to reduce enzymatic browning

Bratt pan – a large rectangular tilting pan used in commercial kitchens for shallow/deep frying, boiling, braising or stewing

Buddhism – a religion. Most Buddhists are vegetarian.

Bulking – flour gives structure/bulk to a baked product

Calcium – a mineral element which is essential for strong bones and teeth

Caramelisation – this happens when sugar is heated

Carbon footprint – a measure of the impact human activities have on the environment in terms of the amount of greenhouse gasses produced through the outlet of carbon dioxide

Cholesterol – produced by the liver and transported round the body as a soft wax

Coagulate – to set

Coeliac disease – a medical condition caused by an allergy to the protein gluten present in the cereals wheat, barley and rye

Collagen – protein found in meat

Complex carbohydrates – carbohydrates that provide a slow release of energy

Component – an individual part that makes up a product

Conduction – heat transferred from one molecule to another

Connective tissue – surrounds the muscle fibres

Contaminated – when foods are infected with micro-organisms and therefore are not safe to eat

Continuous flow production – computer-controlled production method used to produce one specific product in large quantities, non-stop 24 hours a day

Convection – where warm molecules rise and the cooler molecules fall closer to the source of heat

Critical control points – point in the production process that is essential to control

Cross-contamination – the transference of bacteria from raw to cooked foods

Dehydration – a medical condition resulting from insufficient water in the diet

Dental caries – tooth decay

Design specification – the general criteria for a product to be developed

Diabetes – a metabolic disorder caused by the poor absorption of glucose

Dietary fibre – material from plants, which is not digested by humans but which absorbs water and binds other residues in the intestine

Dietary guidelines – advice from the government on recommended food intake in order to achieve dietary goals

Dietary reference values (DRVs) – estimates of the amounts of nutrients needed for good health

Disaccharide – two monosaccharides combined

Disinfection – cleaning with a chemical (cleaning agent) to kill or reduce micro-organisms to an acceptable level to maintain the highest hygienic standards

Diverticular disease – a disease caused by lack of fibre in the diet

Dormant – bacterial growth is slowed down and becomes inactive. Bacteria are not destroyed

Due diligence – care taken when examining and evaluating risks

Eatwell Plate – a model of healthy eating to encourage people to eat the correct proportions of food to achieve a balanced diet

Emulsion – a mixture of two liquids

Energy balance – the relationship between energy input and energy used by the body

Enzymes – proteins which speed up chemical reactions

Essential amino acids – amino acids that cannot be made by the body

Essential fatty acids – small unit of fat that must be supplied in the diet

Estimated average requirement (EARs) – the average amount of a nutrient needed

Ethical Trading Initiative – a group of companies which promote safe working conditions for their employees. This means that the employees have basic labour rights and that they also take care to protect the environment in the packaging and transporting of their products

Extraction rate – how much of a whole grain is used

Extrinsic sugar – sucrose added to a product

Fairtrade – guarantees producers get a fair price for their product

Farm assured – guarantees the highest standard of food safety and hygiene, animal welfare and environmental protection

Fat-soluble vitamins – dissolve in fat

Fermentation – when given the right conditions (warmth, moisture, food and time) yeast produces carbon dioxide and alcohol

Fibre – material, mostly from plants, which is not digested by humans but which absorbs water and binds other residues in the intestine, thus aiding the excretion of waste

Food combining – mixing different low biological value proteins to supply all the essential amino acids

Fortification – the addition of nutrients to a food product to enhance its nutritional content

Fortified food products – have vitamins added to improve their nutritional value

Functional foods – have extra health benefits above their basic nutritional value

Gelatinisation – this is what happens to starches and water when cooked together

Genetically modified (GM) – crops in which the genetic structure has been changed

Gluten – protein found in cereals, especially wheat

Green energy – obtained from alternative energy sources that are considered environmentally friendly and non-polluting; the energy generated from natural sources (for example, wind power, solar power, geothermal, hydro power and tidal/wave power)

Halal meat – meat and poultry slaughtered in a particular way so that no blood remains

Hazard Analysis Critical Control Point (HACCP) – a food safety system based on the prevention of hazards

High biological value proteins – proteins that contain all the essential amino acids

High risk foods – foods that spoil in a short amount of time; those most likely to encourage bacterial growth, such as foods high in protein and moisture

Hinduism – a religion in which the cow is sacred; Hindus will not eat beef or any product from slaughtered cows

Homogenisation – involves forcing milk at high pressure through small holes to break up the fat globules in order to spread them evenly throughout the milk and prevent separation of a cream layer

Hydrogenation – the process of adding hydrogen to oils to make them into solid fats

Impermeable – a material which does not allow substances, for example liquids, to pass through and can be made airtight

Improved nutritional profile – for example, adding additives to increase the vitamin content

Intrinsic sugar – contained within the cell walls of plants

Iron – a mineral present in the blood and stored in the liver; prolonged lack of iron leads to anaemia

Islam – a religion in which people do not eat pork or any pork products; Muslims only eat **Halal** meat

Job/craft/one-off production – production method in which one product is made

Judaism – a religion in which 'Kosher' food is eaten. Jews do not eat pork and meat and dairy produce must not be eaten at the same meal

Kilocalorie (Kcal) – a unit of energy used to indicate the energy yield of foods and the energy expenditure by the body

Kilojoule (KJ) – a unit of energy used to show the energy content of foods

Kneading – to work dough by folding, pressing and stretching with the hands

Lacto-ovo vegetarian – will not eat anything that involves killing an animal but will eat animal products

Lactose – a type of carbohydrate found in milk

Landfill sites – where waste is taken to

Lecithin –an emulsifier found in egg yolks

Life-cycle analysis – when the whole of the production process of the food product is considered and the effect it will have on the environment

Lipids – another name for fats and oils

Low biological value (LBV) proteins – proteins that do not contain all the essential amino acids

Low risk foods – foods which have a long shelf life, such as dried foods

Lower Reference Nutrient Intake (LRNI) – the amount of a nutrient that is enough for a very small number of people who have low needs

Macronutrients – proteins, fats and carbohydrates providing the bulk of our diet; needed by the body in large amounts

Maillard reaction – this happens when foods containing proteins and carbohydrates are cooked by dry methods

Mass production – production method in which large numbers of one product are produced

Methane – a powerful greenhouse gas

Micro-organisms – classified as bacteria, mould and yeast

Micronutrients – vitamins and minerals that are needed in small quantities for health

Minerals – substances used by the body to control processes; they form an essential part of body fluids

Modified Atmosphere Packaging (MAP) – packaging containing a mixture of gases which help to preserve food

Monosaccharide – simple sugar

Monounsaturated fats – a fat molecule with one hydrogen space

Mycoprotein – a good source of vegetable protein that is low in fat

Natural resources – resources that are naturally occurring (for example, oil, trees, metal ore)

Non-starch polysaccharide (NSP) – dietary fibre which cannot be digested by the body

Non-renewable energy resources – resources which will eventually run out (for example, coal, gas, petrol)

Nutrients – the part of a food that performs a particular function in the body

Obesity – excessive fatness, measured as a ratio of weight to height

Optimum – the best conditions for micro-organisms to grow

Organic – grown or reared without the use of artificial aids, fertilisers, pesticides and antibiotics

Organoleptic – qualities of food associated with the senses

Oxidisation – occurs when fruit and vegetables are cut and the cells are exposed to the air

Pathogenic bacteria – harmful bacteria which can cause food poisoning

Perishables – foods that have a short shelf life and that must be stored in the fridge

pH – measurement used to express the acidity or alkalinity of a product

Plaque – build up of bacteria on teeth

Pollution – contamination of soil, water or the atmosphere by harmful substances

Polysaccharide – complex carbohydrate, either starch or fibre

Polyunsaturated fats – a fat molecule with more than one hydrogen space

Primary recycling – the second-hand use of products

Primary research – research collected by yourself

Product specification – very specific characteristics which a product must have

Protein – required for growth, repair and energy

Pureeing – to rub fruit/vegetables through a sieve or process in a blender to form a soft cream paste or thick liquid

Quality assurance – 'a level of guarantee' or 'positive declaration'

Quality assurance system – a system which lays down procedures for making a safe, quality product

Quality control – checking standards of a food product as it is being designed, manufactured and at the end of manufacture

Radiation – heat is passed by electromagnetic waves from one place to another

Rastafarianism – a religion in which members eat food that is natural and clean; Rastafarians do not eat pork and only eat fish that are longer than 30 cm; they cook with coconut oil and do not drink alcohol, milk or coffee

Recyclable – made from materials that can be used again, such as glass or paper

Reference nutrient intake (RNI) – the amount of a nutrient that is enough for most people

Satiety – a feeling of fullness

Saturated fats – come mainly from animal sources and are solid at room temperature

Secondary or physical recycling – waste materials are recycled into different types of products

Secondary research – research collected by other people

Sensory analysis – tasting/testing food products to monitor organoleptic qualities so modifications (changes)/ improvements can be made and products can be matched against design/product specifications

Shorten – fat is used to give a baked product a crisp or crumbly texture

Sikhism – Sikhs have similar eating habits to Hindus

Staple foods – a food that forms the basis of a traditional diet, for example, wheat, barley, rye, maize or rice

Sucrose – sugar found in sugar beet and cane

Tertiary or chemical recycling – products are broken down and reformulated

Textured vegetable protein (TVP) – protein made from soya beans

Vacuum packing – air is removed and the package sealed

Vegan – strict vegetarian who will not eat any animal products; they avoid foods that may have caused an animal pain

Visible and invisible fats – some fats can be seen but mainly they are part of a product and cannot be seen

Water-soluble vitamins – dissolve in water

Index